*Where Shall My*
*Wond'ring Soul Begin?*

# *Where Shall My Wond'ring Soul Begin?*

## THE LANDSCAPE OF EVANGELICAL PIETY AND THOUGHT

*Edited by*

Mark A. Noll and Ronald F. Thiemann

WILLIAM B. EERDMANS PUBLISHING COMPANY
GRAND RAPIDS, MICHIGAN / CAMBRIDGE, U.K.

© 2000 Wm. B. Eerdmans Publishing Co.

255 Jefferson Ave. S.E., Grand Rapids, Michigan 49503 /

P.O. Box 163, Cambridge CB3 9PU U.K.

Printed in the United States of America

05  04  03  02  01  00     7  6  5  4  3  2  1

ISBN  0-8028-4639-4

# Contents

# CONTENTS

# *Preface*

The establishment at Harvard Divinity School of the Alonzo L. McDonald Family Professorship in Evangelical Theological Studies and the inaugural conference in 1998 that produced these essays marked an important and long overdue moment in the history of the School.

Since the early nineteenth century, Harvard Divinity School has been a symbol of liberal Protestant Christianity in the United States. The institutional reality, of course, has always been more complex and less tidy than that.

At the same time that the School was regarded over the decades as a bastion of anti-evangelical liberalism, it attracted a long and steady line of evangelical students. It produced across the disciplines more professors who teach at evangelical seminaries than any other university divinity school in the country.

This is not to dispute the point that evangelical students have always been a minority at the Divinity School. But they have come, they have flourished, and they are some of the graduates of whom we are most proud. Yet the School's evangelical history and tradition have never been lifted up symbolically. The endowment of the McDonald chair provided an opportunity to do so and to establish evangelicalism at Harvard as a serious and ongoing area of academic inquiry.

The purpose of the McDonald chair ("to promote the study of evangelicalism as defined by a set of practices, ideals, convictions, and habits that have characterized a number of Christian traditions over the centuries") inspired the colloquium on "Understanding Evangelicalism" that produced this book. The essays collected here retain the flavor of papers read at a conference, and as they demonstrate, the event was a significant moment not only for Harvard but also for the study of evangelical Christianity itself. The discussion made apparent evangelicalism in all its diversity. Scholars joined together to examine evangelicalism's shared religious features, its intellectual agenda, and the impact its deeply felt religious commitments have had on society, as well as to air differences in a setting of mutual understanding. The Divinity School was able to serve as the place for a new conversation to emerge, one with the evangelical tradition as a partner in a community of diverse theological voices at Harvard.

At the beginning of the colloquium, Mark Noll, the first incumbent of the McDonald Chair and co-editor of this volume, reminded us that in 1740, Harvard College welcomed the itinerant evangelist George Whitefield when he preached in Cambridge. Whitefield concluded that "discipline at Harvard is at a low ebb, and bad books are becoming fashionable among the tutors and students." (He later apologized for this opinion, and by the 1760s, when relations had improved considerably, he helped raise money to replace Harvard books lost in a library fire.)

I am grateful to Mark for the time he spent in Cambridge, for his guidance in organizing the colloquium, and especially for his inaugural lecture. Its title, "Evangelicalism at Its Best," describes not only his topic and the theme of this book but also his own position in the field.

I wish also to acknowledge with gratitude the scholars whose work is represented here. Special mention needs to be made as well of all those who contributed to coordinating the colloquium so successfully and bringing this volume into print: Nancy Birne, Shaun Casey, Sarah Coakley, Harvey Cox, Missy Daniel, William Hutchison, and Susan Sherwin.

It remains only to thank Al McDonald, a deeply committed evangelical Christian and a man of genuine spiritual insight and imagination. His conviction that Harvard would profit from a professorship "to cultivate an understanding of the history, theology, spirituality, and ecumenical practice of evangelical Christianity" made this moment in the history of the Divinity School possible, and we are most grateful.

RONALD F. THIEMANN
Cambridge, Massachusetts

# Evangelicalism at Its Best

## MARK A. NOLL

Evangelicalism at its best is the religion displayed in the classic evangelical hymns. The canon of evangelical hymnody is open, which means that before very long at least a few of the psalms, hymns, and spiritual songs being composed in such lively profusion in contemporary evangelical churches will be added to that canon. As they are added, they will take their place alongside three distinct layers of hymnody that, more than any other expression, define the modern evangelical movement at its best.

When did modern evangelicalism arise in the English-speaking world? We may date that beginning to Jonathan Edwards's preaching on justification by faith in his Northampton, Massachusetts, church in 1735, or to John Wesley's Aldersgate experience in May 1738, or to George Whitefield's momentous preaching tour of New England in September 1740. But as an indication of fresh religious sensibility and in a form that would both guide and inspire the experience of multiplied millions of believers to come, it makes more sense to date the emergence of modern evangelicalism to an act of composition by Charles Wesley. The very week that his brother John received an unusual manifesta-

1

tion of divine grace during the Moravian meeting at Aldersgate, Charles Wesley underwent a similar experience.

Many know what John Wesley wrote in his journal after his experience: "About a quarter before nine, while [the speaker] was describing the change which God works in the heart through faith in Christ, I felt my heart strangely warmed. I felt I did trust in Christ, Christ alone, for my salvation; and an assurance was given me that He had taken away *my* sins, even *mine*, and saved *me* from the law of sin and death." Many, many more have sung the words that Charles composed:

> Where shall my wond'ring soul begin?
>> How shall I all to heaven aspire?
> A slave redeemed from death and sin,
>> A brand plucked from eternal fire.
> How shall I equal triumphs raise,
>> Or sing my great Deliverer's praise?
>
> . . . . . .
>
> Come, O my guilty brethren, come,
>> Groaning beneath your load of sin;
> His bleeding heart shall make you room,
>> His open side shall take you in.
> He calls you now, invites you home,
>> Come, O my guilty brethren, come.

If you doubt the weight of Charles Wesley's contribution to the emergence of modern evangelicalism, ask yourself how many of the words of Edwards, Whitefield, or John Wesley you can quote, and then reflect on how much of Charles Wesley is stored away, not only in your brain but in your heart:

Hark, the herald angels sing,
    Glory to the new-born King . . .
Mild he lays his glory by,
    Born that man no more may die . . .

Jesu, Lover of my soul, Let me to thy bosom fly . . .

Arise, my soul, arise; shake off thy guilty fears;
The bleeding Sacrifice in my behalf appears . . .

Love divine, all loves excelling,
    joy of heaven to earth come down . . .

Come, Thou long-expected Jesus,
    Born to set Thy people free,
From our fears and sins release us,
    Let us find our rest in Thee . . .

Ye servants of God, Your Master proclaim,
And publish abroad His wonderful name:
The name all-victorious of Jesus extol;
His kingdom is glorious and rules over all . . .

"Christ the Lord is risen today,"
    Sons of men and angels say!
Raise your joys and triumphs high:
    Sing, ye heavens; thou earth reply.

The hymns of Charles Wesley and his contemporaries like John Newton, Anne Steele, William Cowper, and William Williams (Pantecelyn) mark the first great outpouring of evangelical hymnody. The second appeared during the remarkable expansion of evangelicalism throughout Britain, Canada, and the United States during the first two-thirds of the nineteenth century. Like the first wave, the classic hymns of the evangelical nineteenth century featured redemptive encounter with the living Christ described through images, tropes, metaphors, and quotations from the Bible. Evangelicalism always involved more than Christ-centered, biblically normed religious experience. But for leaders and followers alike, especially in day-to-day ordinary experience, that kind of piety remained the defining center of the evangelical movements.

In the North Atlantic countries, massive efforts in evangelism, voluntary social reform, and the refinement of taste led to something like an evangelical cultural hegemony. In the United States, for example, the sway of evangelicalism can be noted by the intensely revivalistic tone of religious life manifested in both armies and on both home fronts during the Civil War, and also by the way in which public political discourse developed along lines marked out by itinerating evangelical preachers and evangelical voluntary societies — in other words, by the features of American life that so impressed visitors like Alexis de Tocqueville. But a more intimate and quotidian measure of nineteenth-century evangelical cultural influence is found in the incredible popularity of the hymns of Fanny Crosby of Brooklyn, New York. Among the approximately 8,500 hymns that this blind author wrote, dozens became defining emblems of evangelical experience:

Tell me the story of Jesus, write on my heart every word . . .

All the way my Savior leads me;
    what have I to ask beside?
Can I doubt his tender mercy,
    who through life has been my guide? . . .

Blessed assurance, Jesus is mine!
    O what a foretaste of glory divine!

4

Heir of salvation, purchase of God,
    born of his Spirit, washed in his blood.
This is my story, this is my song,
    praising my Savior all the day long.

In an American world very different from the refinement of Brooklyn Heights, a similar process was at work among those whom an ethical malignancy had made into America's hewers of wood and drawers of water. The decades between the American War for Independence and the Civil War witnessed an accelerating evangelization of African Americans, both slave and free. When allowed, churches were formed, and blacks exerted great energy in learning to read the Bible. Where allowed or not allowed, African Americans sang of their faith. The most distinctive form of that singing was the spiritual. Although authorship, origin, and exact distribution of many spirituals seem to lie beyond historical recovery, by mid-century the spiritual had become a sturdy anchor of African-American religion. The life course reflected in those spirituals was very different from the world in which Fanny Crosby lived. But one thing was similar: the use of biblical materials focused on the omnicompetence of Jesus Christ:

What ship is this that's landed at the shore!
    Oh, glory hallelujah!
It's the old ship of Zion, hallelujah! . . .
What kind of Captain does she have on board?
    Oh, glory hallelujah!
King Jesus is the Captain, hallelujah. . . .

In that morning, true believers, In that morning,
We will sit aside of Jesus, In that morning,
If you should go fore I go, In that morning,

5

You will sit aside of Jesus, In that morning,
True believers, where your tickets, In that morning,
Master Jesus got your tickets, In that morning.

It was the same in Canada. If anything, Protestant evangelical influence was manifest even more strongly and in more ways throughout the Maritimes and Ontario than in the United States. Yet more than the shaping of churches, schools, and public discourse, evangelicalism in nineteenth-century Canada could be defined by the hymns it produced. None of them touched more lives than a hymn written by Joseph Scriven, who, in its words, was reflecting on the dislocation and personal tragedies that had attended his migration from Ireland to Port Hope, Ontario:

What a Friend we have in Jesus,
    All our sins and griefs to bear!
What a privilege to carry
    Everything to God in prayer! . . .
Are we weak and heavy-laden,
    Cumbered with a load of care?
Precious Savior, still our refuge,
    Take it to the Lord in prayer.
Do thy friends despise, forsake thee?
    Take it to the Lord in prayer.
In his arms He'll take and shield thee,
    Thou wilt find a solace there.

Nineteenth-century Britain was an arena in which evangelicalism interacted deeply with conceptions of political economy; where different kinds of evangelical faith virtually monopolized the dissenting churches and also exerted a powerful influence in the Church of England, the Church of Ireland, and the Church of Scotland; and where evangelicals probably contributed more than any other source to the constitution of Victorian sensibility. In such a venue of multivalent evangelical activity, still nothing spoke more directly of the spirituality that undergirded evangelical public life than the hymn. Horatius Bonar, who gave up his parish to join the Scottish Free Church in 1843, was one of the most eminent of those hymn writers, and most of his best-known hymns reiterated for a new era what were already classical evangelical themes:

> Not what these hands have done
> > can save this guilty soul;
> Not what this toiling flesh has borne
> > can make my spirit whole. . . .
> Thy work alone, O Christ,
> > can ease this weight of sin;
> Thy blood alone, O Lamb of God,
> > can give me peace within. . . .
> Thy grace alone, O God,
> > to me can pardon speak;
> Thy power alone, O Son of God,
> > can this sore bondage break.

Yet none of Bonar's hymns, popular as they are, has spoken to and for so many evangelicals as words written in the early 1830s by Charlotte Elliott (1789-1871), sister of an evangelical clergyman in the Church of England, cousin of the missionary activist Henry Venn, and friend of the Geneva evangelical leader H. A. César Malan:

> Just as I am, without one plea,
> > But that Thy Blood was shed for me,
> And that Thou bidst me come to Thee,
> > O Lamb of God, I come.

Elliott's evocation of the language of the Authorized Version, her hymn's reminder of the freighted significance of saintly women (usually slightly in the background), and its quintessentially evangelical mixture of christocentric self-resignation and spiritual self-assertion — all of these are powerfully succinct markers of the evangelicalism that flourished so widely in the English-speaking world in its heyday of cultural influence during the first two-thirds of the nineteenth century.

   It was the same in the third wave of classic evangelical hymnody that produced the gospel song around the turn of the twentieth century. For white evangelicals, Ira Sankey led the way. As D. L. Moody's song leader, Sankey was an indispensable contributor to Moody's phenomenal success in England, Scotland, Canada, and the United States. But much more than anything Moody ever wrote, Sankey's songs long continued to speak of powerful evangelical sentiments:

> There were ninety and nine that safely lay
>   In the shelter of the fold,
> But one was out on the hills away,
>   Far off from the gates of gold. . . .
> [N]one of the ransomed ever knew
>   How deep were the waters crossed;
> Nor how dark was the night that the Lord passed through
>   Ere he found his sheep that was lost.

The black counterpart to Ira Sankey was Charles A. Tindley, who through patience, persistence, and tireless promotion convinced large numbers of African-American churches to enrich their singing with new hymns adjusted to a new era. Tindley is best known for a song published in 1916 that was later amalgamated with the spiritual "I'll Be All Right" and sung to the tune of the latter spiritual as an anthem of the civil rights movement in the 1960s and '70s. In its original version, the hymn's most telling effect was to demonstrate continuity with the Christ-centered emphasis of earlier evangelicalism:

> This world is one great battlefield, With forces all arrayed;
> If in my heart I do not yield I'll overcome some day. . . .
> Tho' many a times no signs appear Of answer when I pray,
> My Jesus says I need not fear, He'll make it plain some day.
> I'll be like Him some day, I'll be like Him some day.

As is clear from even the few hymns I have quoted from the three great eras of evangelical hymnody, these classics defined, with an unusual degree of unanimity, the essence of evangelicalism. Whatever their many differences of theology, ethnicity, denomination, class, taste, politics, or churchmanship (and in these areas divisions existed beyond number), evangelical hymn writers and hymn singers pointed to a relatively cohesive religious vision.

Driving that vision was a peculiarly evangelical understanding of the Trinity. The holiness of God provided occasion for worship but even more a standard that revealed human sinfulness, human guilt, and human need for a savior. At the heart of the evangelical hymnody was Jesus Christ, whose love offered to sinners mercy, forgiveness, and reconciliation with God. In this savior redeemed sinners found new life in the Holy Spirit, as well as encouragement in that same Spirit to endure the brokenness, relieve the pain, and bind up the wounds of a world that the great evangelical hymn writers almost always depicted in strikingly realistic terms.

The classic evangelical hymns, in other words, contain the clearest, the most memorable, the most cohesive, and the most widely repeated expressions of what it meant to be an evangelical. But why regard the religion of these hymns as evangelicalism *at its best*? The answer probably has as much to do with ancient under-

9

standings of Christianity as with contingencies of recent centuries. Conflicts with Roman officials, internal battles over the character of the faith, strenuous apologetics against Jews and pagans, and in time learned discourses exegeting and synthesizing scripture all played their part in the emergence of Christianity during the first centuries after Christ. Wise commentators long since, however, have realized that the *lex credendi* was the *lex orandi,* that the way the church formally defined itself depended ultimately on what and how the church prayed.

Similarly, for the evangelical tradition, great diligence in preaching, an incredible organizational energy, and more learned theology than evangelicals and the critics of evangelicals have recognized went into the creation of modern evangelicalism. But nothing so profoundly defined the *lex credendi* of evangelicalism as the *lex cantandi;* what evangelicals have been is what we have sung.

Just as in the early church, the *lex orandi,* the law of prayer, did not guarantee that the early Christians would live up to the sublime faith expressed in their liturgies, so too with modern evangelicals the possession of a *lex cantandi,* a law of song, has not guaranteed that evangelical practice lives up to the Christ-centered, biblical piety about which evangelicals sing. In the early church, the liturgy, constructed primarily from the words and concepts of scripture, defined a religion of beauty, charity, serenity, magnanimity, holiness, and realistic hope that far outshone the often tawdry realities of actual church practice. So too the hymnody of evangelicalism, perhaps because it so obviously is a creature of the Bible's salvific themes, defined a religion that was clearer, purer, better balanced, and more sharply focused than much evangelical practice. The religion of the classic evangelical hymns is evangelicalism at its best, we might say, because Christian movements in general are at their best in worship, prayer, and hymn.

The classic hymns display evangelicalism at its best in three specific ways. First, a Christ-centered picture of redemption is the scarlet thread running through these hymns. This picture of redemption insists upon the death of Christ on the cross as the only ultimate source of human salvation. What makes the hymns evangelicalism at its best is that in them the boundary of offense is restricted narrowly to the scandal of the cross. Second, the classic evangelical hymns, as well as more general evangelical practice with respect to hymnody, define an unusually broad, unexpectedly gracious ecumenism. Third, the social vision that constitutes a prominent subtheme in the classic evangelical hymns evokes a remarkably winsome vision of altruistic Christian charity.

## The Scandal of the Cross

The history of modern evangelicalism could be written as a chronicle of calculated offense. Those who know even a little evangelical history know how prone evangelicals have been to violate decorum, compromise integrity, upset intellectual balance, and abuse artistic good taste. In specifically theological terms, the evangelical movement, including many of its subcanonical hymns, offers the spectacle of a luxurious expanse of weeds, with multiple varieties of Gnosticism, Docetism, Manicheanism, modalism, and wild eschatological speculation, not to speak of confusion over the *communicatio idiomatum* and manifold outbreaks of unintended Unitarianism, springing up as a threat to the good seed of Nicene and Chalcedonian orthodoxy.

The great hymns are not like that. They do not meander theologically. Whatever else they may lack, they possess the virtue of clarity. In turn, by focusing on the great hymns of evangelicalism, proponents, opponents, and the merely curious can see clearly the essence of evangelicalism with a minimum of distraction. That essence is the central theme in a vast panoply of classic hymns.

Professor Stephen Marini of Wellesley College has twice in recent years tallied the most often reprinted hymns in American Protestant hymnbooks from the colonial era to the decades after World War II. Because of the different range of hymnals he sampled for the two surveys, he has come up with two different hymns as the most often reprinted in American Protestant history. Because the message of one of the hymns is so often repeated in so many of the other classic hymns of evangelicalism, its compact, forceful lines are an especially good record of the center of evangelical concern. That hymn appeared in 1776, and I say with calculated awareness of what else was going on then in Philadelphia and in Scotland, where Adam Smith published his *Wealth of Nations,* that of all world-historical occurrences in that year the publication of August Montagu Toplady's hymn may have been the most consequential:

> Rock of Ages, cleft for me,
> > Let me hide myself in Thee;
> Let the water and the blood,
> > From Thy riven side which flowed,
> Be of sin the double cure,
> > Cleanse me from its guilt and power.

> Not the labours of my hands
> > Can fulfil Thy law's demands;
> Could my zeal no respite know,
> > Could my tears for ever flow,
> All for sin could not atone:
> > Thou must save, and Thou alone.

> Nothing in my hand I bring,
> > Simply to Thy Cross I cling;

Naked, come to Thee for dress;
    Helpless, look to Thee for grace;
Foul, I to the fountain fly;
    Wash me, Saviour, or I die.

Toplady's theme was never put more succinctly, with more theological acumen and greater dramatic power, than in a hymn Charles Wesley wrote at the very beginning of the evangelical movement:

And can it be that I should gain
    An interest in the Savior's blood?
Died he for me, who caused his pain?
    For me? Who him to death pursued?
Amazing love! How can it be
    That thou, my God, shouldst die for me?
'Tis myst'ry all: th'Immortal dies!
    Who can explore his strange design?

Long my imprisoned spirit lay,
    Fast bound in sin and nature's night.
Thine eye diffused a quick'ning ray;
    I woke; the dungeon flamed with light.
My chains fell off, my heart was free,
    I rose, went forth, and followed thee.
No condemnation now I dread,
    Jesus, and all in him, is mine.
Alive in him, my living head,
    And clothed in righteousness divine,
Bold I approach th'eternal throne,
    And claim my crown, through Christ my own.

It is impossible to illustrate quickly the fixation of evangelical hymnody on the saving death of Christ. It is a prominent theme even in many songs written specifically for children:

> Jesus loves me, this I know, For the Bible tells me so. . . .
> Jesus loves me! He who died Heaven's gate to open wide;
> He will wash away my sin, Let his little child come in.

It remained a fixture in the memorable, though more sentimental hymns of the Victorian era, as from Philip P. Bliss:

> "Man of Sorrows," what a name
>     for the Son of God, who came
> Ruined sinners to reclaim!
>     Hallelujah! What a Savior!
> Bearing shame and scoffing rude,
>     in my place condemned he stood;
> Sealed my pardon with his blood:
>     Hallelujah! What a Savior!

Or Horatio G. Spafford's "It Is Well with My Soul":

> My sin — O, the bliss of this glorious thought,
> My sin — not in part but the whole,
> Is nailed to the cross and I bear it no more:
> Praise the Lord, praise the Lord, O my soul!

Even in the much more therapeutic concerns of the modern praise chorus, emphasis upon the redemption won by Christ on the cross is by no means absent.

The classic evangelical hymns do not offend on doctrines of the church and the sacraments, because they touch on these matters only indirectly, if at all. Neither do they offend by promoting the particular doctrines of a faction. The Arminian Charles Wesley and the Calvinist A. M. Toplady both wrote hymns excoriating the theological positions of the other. These hymns died long before their authors, while compositions like "Rock of Ages" and "And Can It Be" are found in the hymnals of almost all Protestants and, since the 1970s, some Roman Catholics as well. While the great hymns everywhere betray implicit trust in the scripture, they do not offend by insisting on a particular definition of biblical authority. Again, the classic evangelical hymns have virtually no politics. Charles Wesley thought the American Revolution was sinful through and through, but American patriots hardly noticed as they went on reprinting his hymns in edition after edition.

I could go on. Different evangelicals of different sorts and at different times have tolerated or advocated racism. They have cheered attacks on the intellect, indulged unimaginable vulgarity in the production of religious kitsch, acted callously to the dispossessed, confused their political allegiances with divine mandates, equated middle-class decorum with sanctification in the Holy Spirit, and tried to pass off gratuitous nonsense as if it were gospel truth — as Toplady, for example, did in the essay where he first published "Rock of Ages" by claiming that the average number of sins committed by each individual in his or her lifetime was 2,522,880,000.

Such failings, as well as the particular dogmas and practices insisted upon by different evangelical churches, have been the occasion for oceans of offense. Whether all or some of these offenses are justified is an open question deserving a degree of serious attention.

The classic evangelical hymns, by contrast, are virtually innocent of such offenses. Rather, their overriding message and the single offense upon which they insist is compacted into the four words that best summarize their message: *Jesus Christ Saves Sinners*. These hymns, in other words, proclaim a particular redemption of substitutionary atonement through a particular act of God accomplished in the particularities of the birth, life, death, resurrection, ascension, and kingly rule of Jesus Christ.

Evangelicalism at its best is an offensive religion. It claims that you cannot be reconciled to God, understand the ultimate purposes of the world, or live a truly virtuous life unless you confess your sin before the living God and receive new life in Christ through the power of the Holy Spirit. Such particularity has always been offensive (see 1 Corinthians 1), and in the multicultural, postmodern world in which we live it is more offensive than ever. But when evangelicalism is at its best, as it is in its greatest hymns, that declaration of a particular salvation is its one and only offense.

## The Ecumenism of the Gospel

Evangelicals, in point of historical fact, may never have been as factious, fissiparous, and sectarian as is commonly thought. To be sure, leaders of evangelical groups have indulged in their fair share of backstabbing, power-mongering, petty-minded polemicizing, gratuitous boundary-marking, and schismatic devilment. Although I am convinced that lay evangelicals have done better than their leaders in preserving the unity of the body of Christ, there is enough fragmentation in the evangelical world to go around for all. I have often heard said in my circles what is no doubt said about different issues in other communions as well: the presence of three confessional Presbyterians guarantees at least four potentially schismatic opinions on the doctrine of predestination.

Evangelicalism at its best, however, embodies a kind of gospel ecumenism that, while it does not overcome the fragmentation to which evangelicalism is prone, nonetheless speaks forcefully against it. In this case, evangelical hymnody has been more an eschatological sign of a unity to come than of a unity realized. Specifically, it is not so much the message of the hymns as how they are used that displays most clearly their ecumenical potential.

John Wesley, for example, eventually broke with the Moravians: they were too passive, too mystical, perhaps too cheerful. But he did not hesitate to translate a few of their hymns. The result is that generations of evangelicals to this day have joined their voices in singing the cooperative efforts of Charles Wesley the Methodist and Nicholas von Zinzendorf the Moravian long after the Moravians and Methodists went their separate ways. And what they have sung is, "Jesus, thy blood and righteousness/ My beauty are, my glorious dress."

Some of the ecumenism of the great evangelical hymns bridges even wider chasms. At the end of the nineteenth century, many evangelicals still regarded the pope as Antichrist and, if they thought of it at all, considered the Oxford Movement but a way station toward Rome. Yet within the same generation that they were written, John Henry Newman's "Lead Kindly Light" and John Keble's "Sun of My Soul, Thou Savior Dear" were being sung by evangelicals. Moreover, a translation by the evangelical Presbyterian James Waddel Alexander of Paul Gerhardt's German translation of Bernard of Clairvaux's "O Sacred Head, Now Wounded" had become a fixture in evangelical hymnbooks.

It is also ecumenically significant to ponder the translating history of Martin Luther's "Ein Feste Burg," the very Marseilles hymn of the Reformation that English-speaking evangelicals were also singing widely by the end of the nineteenth century. Two of the most popular translations of that great hymn were in fact made by individuals whose theological convictions would have excluded them from leadership in almost all evangelical churches — George McDonald, a renegade Scottish Congregationalist run off into Universalism, and Frederick Henry Hedge, a graduate of Harvard Divinity School and promoter of Unitarianism as a pastor and professor.

The ecumenism of the classic evangelical hymns extends beyond ecclesiastical division to the polarities of gender and race as well. Although these hymns follow the conventions of their day in using masculine pronouns for all humans, they do not promote gender wars, and only a lunatic fringe of evangelicals has ever scrupled at not only singing but singing with enthusiasm the hymns of Fanny Crosby, Charlotte Elliott, Frances Ridley Havergal, Carolina Sandell, Cecil Frances Alexander, and Margaret Clarkson.

Race, the most intractable divider of Christians in the modern West, yet is not intractable enough to completely stifle the gospel ecumenism of evangelical hymnody. Many of us whitebread evangelicals act uncomfortable in black churches, and I suspect that many African Americans feel the same in white churches. Yet the white folk still try to sing "A Little Talk with Jesus Makes It Right" or Thomas A. Dorsey's "Precious Lord, take my hand, lead me on, let me stand, I am tired, I am weak, I am worn. Through the storm, through the night, lead me on, to the light, take my hand precious Lord, lead me home."

Hymn-inspired racial inclusiveness goes way back in evangelical history. It was there in 1792, when eleven hundred African Americans — some refugees from slavery in America, others escaping social harassment in a marginally freer Nova Scotia — waded ashore off the West African coast onto a strip of land purchased for their use by the British evangelicals of the Clapham Sect. As they came ashore, so it is said, the settlers joined their voices in Isaac Watts's "Awake, and sing the song of Moses and the Lamb," a hymn drawing on both Testaments and bearing great significance in that hour.

On Whitsunday in 1862, when five thousand South Sea Islanders from Tonga, Fiji, and Samoa gathered to inaugurate a new specifically Christian government with a professedly Christian king, they marked the occasion with a hymn that had become the missionary beacon of the evangelical movement. The consequences of Western imperialism have always been mixed, but it was the Islanders' own choice to appropriate an expressly evangelical gift to mark that day, as they sang Isaac Watts's Christianized version of Psalm 72:

> Jesus shall reign where'er the sun
> Doth his successive journeys run;
> His kingdom stretch from shore to shore
> Till moons shall wax and wane no more.

Although on ecumenical matters evangelicals have not always been at their best, in the spirit with which the classic evangelical hymns have been put to use, evangelicalism expresses an ecumenical vision shaped by the gospel itself. By so doing they illustrate in a specifically Christian way the truth of a German saying: *Wer spricht mit mir ist mein Mitmensch; wer singt mit mir ist mein Bruder;* that is, the folks I talk to are my fellow human beings; the ones I sing with are family.

## A Social Vision

An important subtheme in the classic evangelical hymns is a persistent concern for the relief of suffering. Although this subtheme is almost never developed systematically or structurally, it is nonetheless there from the first, as in the hymn of Isaac Watts sung by the South Sea Islanders:

> Blessings abound where'er he reigns;
> The prisoner leaps to lose his chains,
> The weary find eternal rest,
> And all the sons of want are blest.

19

As J. R. Watson points out in his fine recent book, *The English Hymn*, "Charles Wesley's hymns are forceful because they contain so many words which are physical: for him the life of a Christian was to be experienced in the body as well as in the soul." Thus, the note struck in Wesley's "O for a thousand tongues to sing" is by no means untypical:

> Hear him, ye deaf, his praise, ye dumb,
>     Your loosen'd tongues employ,
> Ye blind behold your Saviour come,
>     And leap ye lame, for joy.

Nor is the challenge to this-worldly service found elsewhere in Wesley's hymns an oddity:

> A charge to keep I have, A God to glorify;
> A never-dying soul to save, And fit it for the sky:
> To serve the present age, My calling to fulfil;
> Oh, may it all my powers engage, To do my Master's will.

In the Victorian era, Fanny Crosby expressed directly the care that at least some evangelicals showed to those for whom few others cared:

> Rescue the perishing, care for the dying,
> Snatch them in pity from sin and the grave;
> Weep o'er the erring one, lift up the fallen,
> Tell them of Jesus, the mighty to save.
> Rescue the perishing, care for the dying;
> Jesus is merciful, Jesus will save.

At its best, the evangelical desire to rescue the perishing has meant putting the perishing on their feet in the here and now as well as preparing them for eternity. Of course, we evangelicals are often not at our best, so the occasions are many of having been lured away from Christ-inspired social service by prejudice, class consciousness, middle-class fastidiousness, blindness to the structural conditions of power that condition personal choices, and the many other forms of social sinfulness that beset the human race in general.

But at its best, evangelicalism is William Wilberforce, who for the sake of the kingdom of Christ devoted his life to the destruction of slavery. At its best, evangelicalism is the Grande-Ligne Mission of Madame Henriette Feller, who in nineteenth-century Quebec patiently joined Protestant witness to educational exertion. At its best evangelicalism is the tireless, unpretentious, but absolutely stunning social achievements of the Salvation Army and the Mennonite Central Committee. And at its best evangelicalism is the motivation from the Gospel of Matthew that has inspired many to establish shelters for pregnant women in distress and to march on pro-life picket lines: "Come to me, all who labor and are heavy laden, and I will give you rest. Take my yoke upon you, and learn from me; for I am gentle and lowly in heart, and you will find rest for your souls" (Matthew 11:28-29). "Let the children come to me, and do not hinder them; for to such belongs the kingdom of heaven" (Matthew 19:14).

Concern for the terrestrial outworking of the kingdom of God is not as fully developed in the classic evangelical hymns as it should be. But it is indubitably there, reflecting a vision of human need inspired by the love of Jesus and devoted, not to extrinsic social or political causes, but to the good of the ones being served.

The researchable historical question as to when, how, in what proportion, and to what extent evangelicals have functioned at their best is too complex for easy adjudication. As an academic committed to the values of modern historical research when those values function *at their best*, I am reluctant to attempt a quick answer, since there is so much contradictory evidence.

In the history of evangelicalism, for every Jonathan Edwards dedicating the mind to discern the glories of God in the stuff of daily human existence, there are many James Davenports running amuck into mind-denying enthusiasm. For every William Jennings Bryan eager to judge the marketplace by the cross, there is a Russell Conwell eager to bury the cross in an acre of diamonds. For every Johann Albrecht Bengel or Gordon Fee examining issues of biblical interpretation with painstaking care, there are many more evangelicals racing from slipshod plundering of the biblical text to bogus exegetical certainties. For every Wilberforce bringing the resources of evangelical faith to bear for spiritual and terrestrial liberation there is a James Henley Thornwell bringing pretty much the same resources to bear for a now incomprehensible mixture of spiritual liberation and terrestrial enslavement. For every Billy Graham maintaining theological, financial, and sexual integrity as a traveling evangelist, there is a Marjo exploiting kerygmatic charisma for base ends. Or to take trenchant examples from Charles Marsh's captivating study, *God's Long Summer: Stories of Faith and Civil Rights* (1997), about the dramatic civil rights confrontations of 1964 in the state of Mississippi, for every Fannie Lou Hamer who was sustained by thoughts of Jesus as she was being beaten in the Winona, Mississippi, city jail, there is a Sam Bowers, imperial wizard of the White Knights of the Ku Klux Klan, believing that he was defending the sovereignty of God and the resurrection of Jesus Christ by conspiring to murder three civil rights workers.

From a historical perspective, therefore, I am reluctant to conclude too much about the question of whether evangelicals in practice have lived up to the vision of faith and life found in the great evangelical hymns. Yet as a historian who is also an evangelical, I must say more. Even if, historically considered, evangelicals have not always acted at our best, evangelical convictions are not compromised. In fact they may be strengthened.

It is evangelical to insist that humans are redeemed by God's grace rather than by the exercise of their own capacities; it is evangelical to claim that the righteousness on which we rely is a forensic gift rather than a personal possession; it is evangelical to claim that power resides in powerlessness and that the cross is a symbol both for human weakness as well as divine love. Holiness unto the Lord is a prominent evangelical theme, but it rests upon justification by faith alone.

Thus, even if evangelicals have acted at our best only inconsistently, there is nothing in that fact contradicting evangelical conviction. In fact, for evangelicals to confess how far short they have fallen of the divine beauty that they claim to honor is a very important first step toward realizing evangelicalism at its best.

At the end of the twentieth century, all Christians, indeed all humans, have multiple reasons to hope that evangelicalism will be at its best. In the United States, sophisticated surveys suggest that more than a fourth of the national population are active participants in evangelical churches (that is, about the same number as active Roman Catholics and mainline Protestants combined). A recent survey by John N. Vaughan published in his newsletter, *Church Growth Today,* reported that nine out of the ten most rapidly growing non-Catholic churches in the United States, and 93 out of the top 100, identify themselves as evangelical, charismatic, Pentecostal, Southern Baptist, fundamentalist, or by some other label usually considered as fitting under the broader evangelical umbrella.

The situation for world Christianity reveals the same picture. Annual tabulations by the missiologist David Barrett suggest that of the world's nearly 2 billion people identified with

Christian churches, something like 700 million are evangelical in a broad sense of the term (for Barrett, this category also includes some Roman Catholics). His figures make clear that the only varieties of Protestantism growing with any concerted energy in the world are evangelical in general and most likely Pentecostal in particular. Thus, it is important not just for the evangelical community but for the world as a whole that evangelicals live, think, and pray at their best.

That it might in fact be possible to hope for such a prospect is indicated by an account of two last hymns. Christian missions began among the Bor Dinka on the east side of the White Nile River in the southern Sudan in 1906. But for the first seventy years and more of its activity the Anglican Church Missionary Society experienced only scant results. From the 1970s, and with accelerating force in the 1980s and '90s, however, Christianity under the guidance of the Episcopal Church of the Sudan has expanded with remarkable strength. The external circumstances of this expansion are tragic, for the Dinka have been caught in civil war with succeeding Muslim factions from the northern Sudan and have suffered great loss of life and property.

Precisely in those circumstances the Christian faith has taken root but in a distinctively Bor Dinka manner. Everywhere in the new Dinka churches and among the burgeoning tide of converts is seen the cross. The display of the cross is particularly striking in massed processions on holy days when, as described by Marc Nikkel, "their crosses [create] a thick forest, surging with the crowds, thrusting heavenward with every beat of the songs they sing." The prominence of the cross in Bor Dinka life represents a christianization of existing cultural forms, for the Dinka had historically put to use a wide variety of carved walking sticks, staffs, and clubs. Among Dinka converts, the Christian symbol has filled a form provided by traditional culture.

But the Dinka appropriation of the cross has also become a

powerful expression of pastoral theology, expressed in a flourishing of fresh, indigenous hymnody. These hymns reprise historical evangelical emphases by pointing to the cross as a comprehensive reality of great power. The cross provides protection against hostile spirits, or the *jak;* the cross figures large in the baptisms that mark conversions; in hymns the cross becomes an ensign or banner raised high for praise and protection; the cross brings the great God, *Nhialic,* close to the Dinka in the person of Christ, whose suffering is appropriated with striking subjectivity; the cross is spoken of as the *mën,* or the solid central post that supports the Dinka's large, thatched cattle sheds; and the cross becomes a symbol of the potent Spirit who replaces the ancestral *jak,* whose protective powers have so obviously failed in recent years. A song composed by Mary Nyanluaak Lem Bol is only one of the many recent hymns illustrating the depth to which the cross has entered Dinka culture in desperate times:

> We will carry the cross. We will carry the cross.
> The cross is the gun for the evil *jok.*
> Let us chase the evil *jok* away with the cross.

This expression of Bor Dinka faith is in the great tradition of classical evangelical hymnody. It brings the saving work of Christ near; it is a sign of miraculous hope in a dark and threatening world. If such circumstances continue to lead to the writing of such hymns, it may be possible to think that evangelicalism can approximate its best.

In the second survey made by Professor Stephen Marini, "All Hail the Power of Jesus' Name" emerges as the most often reprinted hymn in American Protestant hymnbooks. This hymn's story reveals much that is typical of evangelicalism. As an indication of the kind of ecumenism that flourishes among evangelicals, the version of the hymn most often sung today actually represents an original composition of Edward Perronet, who was a pedobaptist associating primarily with the Methodists, and John Rippon, a Baptist. In addition, the tune "Diadem," the most lively of several tunes to which the hymn is sung, was composed by an eighteen-year-old Wesleyan hat maker, James Ellor.

Less auspiciously, Edward Perronet's career is also not untypical of evangelicalism. Perronet, it turns out, was not an easy chap to get along with. As a young man he eagerly joined in the work of the Wesleys, but his zeal for revival led him to bitter attacks on the Church of England that soon alienated him from the Wesleys, who always saw their work as a complement to official Anglicanism. Perronet next took one of the chapels in the Countess of Huntingdon's Connection, but the violence of his festering anti-Anglicanism remained so strong, he wore out the countess's patience and finally ended up pastoring a Congregational church.

Evangelicalism at its best is not the career of Edward Perronet. Evangelicalism at its best, rather, is the hopes, dedication, aspirations, and longing that have led tens, maybe hundreds of millions of evangelicals to sing, decade after decade, and with all their hearts:

> All hail the power of Jesus' Name;
>> Let Angels prostrate fall;
> Bring forth the royal diadem
>> To crown Him Lord of all. . . .
> Sinners, whose love can ne'er forget
>> The wormwood and the gall,
> Go spread your trophies at His feet,
>> And crown Him Lord of all.
> O that, with yonder sacred throng,
>> We at His feet may fall,
> Join in the everlasting song,
>> And crown him Lord of all.

# Christ-Centered Piety

## DALLAS WILLARD

My approach to the subject of piety rests on the assumption that one of the great engines of individual and social transformation has been evangelical thought and experience. My interest in evangelicalism is not simply in its power as a social phenomenon, but also its power over human existence. For various reasons, a great deal of that power has been lost.

Piety refers to the inward and outward states and acts that constitute a life of devotion — chiefly to God, but commonly also to parents (such as when we speak of "filial piety") and, by a further extension, to any relationship appropriately similar to that of child to parent (when we speak, for example, of a school as our "alma mater"). Externally viewed, piety consists of the routine activities carried out in a sustaining relationship that honors those who give us life and well-being.

In his report for the academic year 1986-87, former Harvard president Derek Bok wrote: "Religious institutions no longer seem as able as they once were to impart basic values to the young. In these circumstances, universities, including Harvard, need to think hard about what they can do in the face of what

27

many perceive as a widespread decline in ethical standards." President Bok went on to say:

> [T]oday's course on applied ethics does not seek to convey a set of moral truths but tries to encourage students to think carefully about complex moral issues. . . . The principal aim of the course is not to impart "right answers" but to make students more perceptive in detecting ethical problems when they arise, better acquainted with the best moral thought that has accumulated through the ages, and more equipped to reason about the ethical issues they will face in their own personal and professional lives.

At the end of the report, he concluded:

> Despite the importance of moral development to the individual student and the society, one cannot say that higher education has demonstrated a deep concern for the problem. . . . especially in large universities, the subject is not treated as a serious responsibility worthy of sustained discussion and determined action by the faculty and administration.

I am a great admirer of Derek Bok, and I regularly use his book *The Cost of Talent* (1993) in a course I teach on the professions in American life. At the conclusion of that book, he notes the quandary over what to do about the unequal distribution of income among the professions, since many of the most important ones (especially teaching and public service) are "starving" on the scale of remuneration. He can only say that we need to change our values.

Where do we go to accomplish that? It is understandable that we should not pay much attention to moral development if there is no basis in knowledge to deal with it. Bluntly put, that is where we stand today. Many intellectuals don't even think of morality as an area of knowledge. Some of the most important books written on the subject of moral values regard it as an area of systematically false or meaningless statements.

The Christ-centered piety of the evangelical tradition provides both the knowledge and the community within which people can find a basis for moral development, because in it they find a basis for human life.

We do not claim that evangelical piety is the only Christ-centered piety. That would be historically mistaken and harmful in many respects. There are many others. One of the first books that Wesley published, for example, was a little version of *The Imitation of Christ* by Thomas à Kempis that was called *The Christian Pattern*. Nevertheless, a clearly identifiable tradition of Christ-centered piety characterizes the evangelical movement, and I want to outline its major aspects.

The three substantive elements of evangelical piety are conviction of sin, conversion, and testimony. Conviction of sin is no longer a popular topic among evangelicals. It has disappeared for the most part, but that is a recent development. Mordecai Ham, the evangelist who converted Billy Graham, preached for weeks before he would give people an opportunity to receive Christ. Often their suffering would become very great. In Savannah, Georgia, it drove Christians to become so burdened that they went downtown and rented empty store buildings in order to hold meetings themselves where they could invite people to receive Christ.

Wesley's famous statement, "I must preach law before I preach grace," was the standard; now it is disregarded. Yet the foundation for evangelical piety remains not only conviction of sin, alienation from God, condemnation, and a sense of eternal loss, but also bondage to sin — the inability to stop sinning. The evangelical tradition, in such figures as Wesley, Richard Baxter, Charles Finney, and many others, deals at great length with this.

Sometimes the tradition verges on perfectionism, one of the ghosts that haunts some forms of evangelicalism. But it is conviction of sin that remains a standard part of Christ-centered piety in the evangelical tradition.

The second basic element is conversion. This involves both reconciliation and regeneration. The loss of the concept of regeneration characterizes much of evangelical theology today. Often all that is stressed is reconciliation or forgiveness. Sometimes the doctrine of regeneration is totally absorbed in the doctrine of justification. But that is not characteristic of the tradition generally. If you read not only the popular sources but also the standard theologies, you will see that regeneration, or coming to a new kind of life, is as central to conversion as forgiveness. Perhaps, indeed, forgiveness is subordinate to it. You are given new life and, in that process, your sins are, of course, forgiven. You can't go along with God without forgiveness.

The third element, testimony, lives on in many quarters of the evangelical movement, but not, by and large, the way it did traditionally, when testimony was often treated as an integral part of conversion, and belief and confession were inseparable.

Beyond these foundational elements of Christ-centered piety in the evangelical tradition, there are some disciplinary aspects — disciplinary because they are thought of (to use Wesley's phrase) as "means of grace" or ways of sustaining and developing one's life. Primary among these are the public ministry of the word of God, individual Bible study, prayer, and the ideal of a whole-life discipline and holiness. Our entire life, no matter what we are doing, is a part of our faith in Christ.

This was a valid transmission of the Lutheran idea of the priesthood of the believer. It did not mean that any believer could do priestly or religious things, but rather that whatever any believer was doing was a priestly act unto God. This belief does descend very clearly through much of the evangelical tradition.

Finally, piety involves making "the fields white unto harvest." This notion has several meanings, including the giving of money and goods. One of the great strengths of Wesley's early little groups was that everyone was supposed to give something, no matter how small. You gave something when you met with your group, and it was used for the benefit of the church as well for those who had needs of any kind.

Making the fields white unto harvest also requires witness. That means speaking individually to others about their condition before God and God's provision for them, as well as involvement in public efforts of evangelization including missionary outreach across the world. Evangelical piety requires presenting the gospel in all of its connections to life as well as in special public efforts to reach out.

The final aspect of making the fields white unto harvest is standing for the truth. This broad category includes "earnestly contending for the faith, once delivered." But it also means standing for what is right and just and good in society, including "speaking truth to power" and political efforts of various kinds.

Those who are living thoughtfully in evangelical circles throughout the generations will very likely believe they have not quite measured up if they are missing any of these areas of activity. For evangelicals, Christ-centered piety must always be from the heart and unto the Lord. It is not for the benefit of appearance. It is not to impress people. It is not to impress God. It is a matter of an honest and transparent heart standing before God and simply calling out, "Just as I am without one plea."

That hymn beautifully expresses this area of transparency, of not trying to make adjustments or impress, but just being who I am and saying that Christ's death on the cross means that now I don't have to be anything other than I am. Since I come to God on such a basis, then I can come to you also and say, "Just as I am without one plea." We deal with one another on that basis. That is evangelical piety at its best. It is not entirely evangelical without qualification, however, and one must include in this definition people like Dietrich Bonhoeffer and others who displayed this attitude of piety. But evangelicals and others do emphasize this kind of transparency as a part of the gospel life.

In evangelical piety, discipleship to Jesus is a process of learning. It means living interactively with his resurrected presence (through his word and through other people) as we progressively learn to lead our lives as he would. One of the primary problems for contemporary evangelicals is that we have lost the concept of discipleship. Among evangelicals generally, it is now assumed that you can be a Christian without being a disciple of Jesus. In fact, this is widely assumed far beyond evangelical circles. To be a disciple is to be an apprentice or student. We even farm discipleship out to parachurch organizations and assume that the local church is not necessarily in that business.

In fact, we are somewhat at a loss as to what discipleship is. That is partly related to some theological developments. The teaching of salvation by grace through faith has, in many quarters, brought people to a condition where they really don't know what they are supposed to do. This is no wonder. My background is Southern Baptist. We will preach to you for an hour that there is nothing you can do to be saved, and then sing to you for a half-hour trying to get you to do something to be saved.

We are not only saved by grace; we are paralyzed by it. There is deep confusion. I like to say that grace is not opposed to effort; grace is opposed to earning. Earning and effort are not the same thing. Earning is an attitude, and grace is definitely opposed to that. But it is not opposed to effort. When you see a person who has been caught on fire by grace, you are apt to see some of the most astonishing efforts you can imagine. Of course, the evangelical tradition is filled with effort — for example, the great missionaries (Judson and Carey and others) who went out. Some would say to them, "Don't you believe God is going to save who he is going to save?" And they would reply, "Yes, that's exactly why I am going. I want to be there when it happens." Grace is a tremendous motivator when you understand it rightly.

Another confusion is that evangelicals often fall into legalism when we try to obey Christ. That is due in large part to the fact that we have emphasized "trying" but not "training." When you try to "bless those who curse you," for example, trying will prove never to be enough; you have to be trained for that. Such training comes under the area of discipleship, but today, generally speaking, we have separated faith in Christ from obedience or fulfillment. There is no bridge to get from one to the other. That bridge is discipleship.

We have lost discipleship largely because in the evangelical tradition we have lost Christ as teacher. The idea of Christ as teacher no longer means much. This has historical roots in the modernist-fundamentalist controversy, when fundamentalists and conservatives began to understand talk of Christ-as-teacher as code words for "he is just a man." There was an inward arming against this idea of Christ as teacher. But, of course, if you don't have a teacher, you can't have any students or disciples.

The idea of spiritual discipline is very rich in the evangelical tradition. Discipline is something we do to enable ourselves to do what we cannot do by direct effort. Yet the idea of discipline disappears in evangelicalism because the teacher has disappeared.

Evangelicals have a long series of problems reclaiming for our time the power of evangelical tradition, thought, and experience as a primary engine to drive the moral transformation of individuals and society. These are tied to the problem of the use of reason and understanding, a problem that also comes to us, in part, as a reaction to the controversies at the end of the last century and the first part of this century. Reason and knowledge were set on the side of the Devil by many evangelicals and by nearly all people who would be called fundamentalist. It was thought that somehow what went wrong with those people over there (the modernists) was that they started thinking. And perhaps they read too many books, possibly in German or French. There was an armament against the idea of reason. Today we must return to this issue in order to capture Christ as teacher and begin to think of him as an intelligent person, which is hard for many people. If you ask someone to list the smartest man in the world, very few people will list Jesus Christ, and that is sad. (If he was divine, would he be dumb?)

Some years ago, there was an ecumenical evangelical effort that went under the heading of "Jesus as Lord." It didn't succeed very well because the whole person of Jesus, which is crucial to Christ-centered piety, was not involved. If you don't think Jesus was smart, what can you mean by calling him Lord? We have to recapture that element.

As we do that, the ideal character of evangelicalism as a life-transforming force begins to reemerge. Then we have reason to think that there might even be some answer to the questions of moral development raised by such important leaders as Derek Bok. He is not alone, of course, in raising those kinds of questions. But where are we to go, if we cannot provide a knowledge of reality and virtue and goodness at a practical level, as has been provided by people in the evangelical tradition?

At the end of his book *The Field of Ethics* (1901), based on the William Belden Noble Lectures for 1899, Harvard philosophy professor George Herbert Palmer listed the names of leaders in the field and concluded: "Ethics is certainly the study of how life may be full and rich, and not, as is often imagined, how it may be restrained and meagre," which, unfortunately, is often the picture that we get of evangelical life. "Those words of Jesus — of which Phillips Brooks was so fond — announcing that he had come in order that men might have life and have it abundantly, are the clearest statement of the purposes of both morality and religion, of righteousness on earth and in heaven."

Evangelical thought and tradition supply us with a content that can be brought into today's world to yield life that is abundant and full. I trust and hope and pray that the occasion of this colloquium, under the leadership of people at Harvard, will open the way to a renewal of that kind of depth of life and thought.

# Commitment to Scripture

## WILLIAM J. ABRAHAM

I feel like a car salesman whose customers are looking for a new Cadillac, but all I have to offer is a battered old Ford. Is there anything new or fresh or worthwhile to say on a topic that has been the cause of endless boredom outside evangelicalism and the occasion for acrimonious controversy within it?

I want to argue that in its treatment of scripture, the great strengths of evangelicalism have been twofold: its readiness to engage the epistemological issues that swirl around scripture, and its persistence in claiming that scripture is an utterly indispensable means of grace for the church as a whole. Moreover, it has exhibited these strengths in what can only be described as an unhealthy intellectual environment.

What does it mean for the church to have a canon of scripture? Is it to have a criterion of theological truth, or is it, more modestly, to have a list of books agreed upon by the church to be read every Sunday in its worship of the triune God? This is an old but much neglected topic, perhaps last taken up in real earnest in the debate between Theodor Zahn and H. W. Beyer in the nineteenth and early twentieth centuries and nicely reviewed by Harry Gamble.[1]

To put it simply, Zahn argued that canon is best understood as a list, and Beyer, that it was a criterion. I think that Zahn was right. Moreover, the shift from canon as list to canon as criterion was one of the most momentous revolutions in the history of the church and Western culture. If we agree with Zahn and think of the canon as a list approved by the church, then the implications are fascinating.

First, we cannot confine canon to scripture. The canon of scripture is part of a wider network of canonical materials, persons, and practices that are central to the life of the church. Thus there was not just a canon of scripture but also a canon (or rule) of truth, a canon of sins, a canon of Fathers, a canon of bishops, even, we might say, a canon of icons, and the like. Few have captured this better than the obscure nineteenth-century French Protestant, Eduard Reuss (1804-1891):

> It must not be forgotten that the use of the term *canon* has never been restricted to the Bible. There were canons of councils, canon law, the canonical life, canons of cathedrals, etc. All these expressions have at bottom the same origin and are derived from a primitive meaning anterior to our canon of scripture.[2]

Second, given this reorientation on what counts as canonical material, we need an appropriate conception of canon to cap-

1. See his *The New Testament Canon: Its Making and Meaning* (Philadelphia: Fortress Press, 1985), pp. 15-18.
2. Eduard Reuss, *History of the Canon of the Holy Scriptures in the Christian Church* (Edinburgh: R. W. Hunter, 1891), p. 218.

ture the nature of the phenomenon to be described. My own proposal, taking a cue from 2 Timothy 3:16, is that we should think of canon in all its forms as essentially a means of grace in the church. The varied canonical heritage of the church is a rich tapestry of materials, persons, and practices given by the Holy Spirit to make us wise unto salvation, to bring us to God, to recreate in us the very mind of Jesus Christ, and to make us holy.

Note that in developing its canonical tradition the church did not canonize any theory of revelation or knowledge. It no more did this than it canonized a theory of atonement or inspiration. This is not to say that its teachers and preachers and members did not have deep convictions on these matters or theories about them. On the contrary, they had all sorts of convictions about these topics. The point is that these were left to be carried in the bosom and midrash of the church. There was no official ruling or listing on these issues.

Why, then, did it become common to reduce canon to scripture and turn it into a criterion? The deepest insights into this were supplied by an even more obscure nineteenth-century thinker, the remarkable Russian theologian Aleksey Stepanovich Khomiakov (1804-1860).[3] When the West added the *filioque* clause to the Nicene Creed, it clearly departed from the canonical doctrine — the rule of faith and the rule of truth — of the church. How is this to be defended? What warrant justifies this change, aside from the fact that it is very bad manners to do this without taking it to the whole church, as Khomiakov points out? Not an appeal to reason, for theology is more than an appeal to naked reason. Nor an appeal to scripture, for to make that move is to read the texts that relate to this issue in the Gospel of John and

---

3. See his "On the Western Confessions of Faith," in Alexander Schmemann, *Ultimate Questions: An Anthology of Modern Russian Thought* (New York: Holt, Rinehart and Winston, 1965), pp. 31-69.

the Book of Acts in such a way that the temporal sending of the Spirit is confused with the eternal relations in the Trinity. We need an entirely different epistemological strategy.

One way to justify the change is to take a single element of the canonical heritage and turn it into an epistemic mechanism. This is precisely what happened. Within the canonical practice of episcopacy, the bishop of Rome was given a privileged position and endowed with the epistemic capacity to identify the final truth in theology. To use a term of Alvin Plantinga, the pope became an epistemic module who, when properly functioning, was infallible in matters of faith and morals. The appeal to papal infallibility is the short and easy way to secure the addition of the *filioque* clause to the Nicene Creed.

Turning the pope into an epistemic module or mechanism was aided and abetted by others. Thus it fit with the urge to have a theory of revelation and inspiration as that related to the canon of scripture. This allowed scripture to be isolated from the rest of the canonical heritage, which in turn was reworked into tradition and then assigned varied weights on an epistemic scale of probability. In fact, the word "probable" prior to the modern period meant "approved by authority."

No one put all this better than Aquinas, who borrowed lavishly from Aristotle and locked the canon of scripture into a complex theory of knowledge featuring a theory of *sola scriptura,* a theory of divine revelation, a theory of probable tradition, and a theory of papal infallibility. It is small wonder that some modern evangelicals have coveted Aquinas's theory of scriptural inerrancy and infallibility. Once we drop the appeal to tradition and papal infallibility, it is the unseen root of the doctrines of the magisterial Reformation.

In all of this we have an intellectual revolution on our hands. The complex, delicate, canonical heritage of the church has now been enmeshed in epistemology. To coin a term, it has been radically epistemized. As a result, the spiritual and intellectual life of the church, mediated through the canonical materials, practices, and persons of the tradition, has become hostage to the philosophy department. The consequences of this for the history of theology have yet to be told, but the boundaries of the road are conspicuously clear.[4] The church and its theologians are now hostage to epistemology. The epistemologists stand sentry at every turn in the road. The current effort by some evangelicals to come to terms with the move from modernity to postmodernity is simply one more effort by the prisoners to placate the regime of the epistemological establishment or the would-be establishment. Not surprisingly, other evangelicals are nervous. Their own competing epistemological proposals are not just the product of their intellectual sweat and labor; they often constitute the evangelical tradition as they live and teach it.

How well has evangelicalism fared in its conception and use of scripture in this hostile environment? If we take evangelicalism in its richest expressions across the centuries, from the Reformation to our own day,[5] and if we take it at its best, then at the epistemological level it has more than held its own in the contest to provide a theory of reflective rationality for the Christian faith.

In some cases, evangelicals have come up with their own interesting suggestions. Thus Calvin's attempt to rework the doctrine of the inner witness of the Holy Spirit as a way of securing the true location of divine revelation in the canon of scripture is

---

4. I have charted the longer narrative on this theme in *Canon and Criterion in Christian Theology: From the Fathers to Feminism* (Oxford: Clarendon, 1998).

5. I have argued that it should be taken in a rich and expansive manner in *The Coming Great Revival: Recovering the Full Evangelical Tradition* (San Francisco: Harper & Row, 1984).

an amazing achievement. To be sure, Calvin is profoundly ambiguous. Is the inner witness an appeal to special revelation in the heart of the believer, or is it a delicate appeal to religious experience? If it is the former, we are arguing in a circle; if the latter, we are preparing the ground for the great liberal Protestant experiment of modernity. We need not decide that issue here. It is enough to draw attention to the creative genius that is at work.

More generally, the strategy in evangelicalism has been one of creative redeployment of the epistemological options of the day. One thinks of Jonathan Edwards and his redeployment of Locke and Berkeley or, less successfully, the effort of John Wesley as a "reasonable enthusiast" to redeploy the work of Locke and his favorite French mystics. In both cases, there was an attempt to keep the Christian faith alive in a world dominated by empiricism.

Surely the greatest experiment in deployment is to be found in the work of the great Princeton theologians of the nineteenth century. In this case, the philosophical materials were mined from the quarry of Thomas Reid and his Scottish common sense realism, imported not once but twice to Princeton. The second time, it came through the philosophy department in Belfast, where I was trained, in the person of James McCosh.[6] This is not the first or last time that the other half of Ireland has made its little contribution to the fortunes of evangelicalism at the international level.

The core of Reid's epistemology is foundationalist. There are basic beliefs (the platitudes of common sense, for example) that we are entitled to hold without evidence. Other beliefs are then secured by their evidential relationship to these foundations.

Immanuel Kant, relying on the prejudicial reading of Joseph

6. The first time around it was brought by John Witherspoon.

Priestly, was profoundly mistaken to dismiss Reid as a hack teacher of common sense. Reid's vision is now rightly seen as one of the jewels of Western epistemology.

What is fascinating is the way this was received and deployed at Princeton. Archibald Alexander followed Reid as an evidentialist in the epistemology of theology. One established the truths of Christianity, first, by appeal to natural theology, and second, by appeal to special revelation secured by miracles.

Charles Hodge appropriated Reid in a radically different way. For Hodge, belief in God, belief in the scriptures, and belief in Christ were all properly basic beliefs that one was entitled to hold without evidence. Arguments for these beliefs were strictly secondary and ancillary. Benjamin Warfield quietly passed all this over and recovered the position of Alexander, bending all his powers to develop a vise-like grip of evidentialism that has been so beloved by many conservative evangelicals.

What is perhaps most interesting in the case of all three Princetonians is that in the midst of their deployment of common sense realism, they lost their nerve and became skeptics in theology. Thus they began their work with the doctrine of the reliability of the senses to fend off Hume and the skeptics, but when they came to scripture, their common sense convictions deserted them, and they insisted that without a completely infallible foundation all is lost in theology.

My aim here is not to identify the flaws but to applaud the intention. Hodge and Warfield valiantly sought to tackle the tough questions that arise in the epistemology of theology. They knew that philosophical work was inescapable, and they sought to bend the options available to them in defense of the gospel. So, too, did their opponents in the Calvinist camp, most notably in a minority report from Holland in the work of Herman Bavinck.

It is, therefore, no surprise that the discipline of philosophy should be thriving on evangelical campuses. Nor is it surprising that philosophers of the stature of Alvin Plantinga and Nicholas Wolterstorff should have arisen within the Reformed wing of evangelicalism. As my mother would say, philosophers do not arise from nowhere, like cabbage heads suddenly appearing on the surface of the river. Like cabbage heads, philosophers have to be planted and grown in appropriate soil.

The garden of evangelicalism has been a fertile field of philosophical endeavor, and it is so today. In my judgment, much remains to be done. We need a richer account of the place of classical foundationalism within the history of evangelical theology, not least in the Reformers as that led in to the beginnings of the Enlightenment. I am calling for a deep rereading of the beginnings of the Enlightenment, relocating it in the debates about the criteria that were, in fact, central to the Reformation and Counter-Reformation.

That is the historical side. On the constructive side, we need a bountiful account of the delicate and revolutionary place of special revelation in the epistemology of theology. It is fair to say, however, that evangelicals have more than held their own in providing various theories of reflective rationality as the gospel has spread into the nooks and crannies of modern culture.

⁂     ⁂

There is another and equally important side to evangelicalism in its approach to scripture. I have in mind the valiant efforts on the part of evangelicals to keep alive the canon of scripture as a pivotal means of grace in the church. In this instance, the great heroes and heroines are not to be found in the intellectual centers of theology, but in the evangelical underworld of bible study groups, movements, fellowships, associations, societies, revival meetings, and the like. The treasures of the tradition in this case are found in the spiritual materials and practices of the tradition

— in preaching, scriptural commentaries, pious calendars, hymnody, gospel songs, love feasts, class meetings, covenant groups, prayer meetings, annual revivals, and the old annual conferences that have now dissolved into bureaucratic meetings. The treasures are to be located in pietism, Methodism, the Society of Quakers, revivalism, the Salvation Army, Pentecostalism, and the modern charismatic movement. The heroes of the tradition are Philipp Spener and August Francke, John Wesley and George Whitefield, Charles Finney and D. L. Moody, William and Catherine Booth, and Fanny Crosby.

In this instance, the effort is made less to deal with the esoteric but important issues of epistemology and truth, and more to engage the popular culture, to convert the lost, to reclaim the nominally Christian, to bring in the millennium, to take the gospel to the ends of the earth, to reform the nation, and to rescue the perishing.

A general brand of what we might call Christian orthodoxy is assumed. For the most part, it is Arminian rather than Calvinist, which is why those in the Reformed and Calvinist tradition don't quite know what to do with it. This really is a kind of evangelical underworld that we would better leave in Texas and Northern Ireland. There is within it a certain impatience with theories of knowledge. If there is a theory of knowledge, it is worked out as Wesley did it — on horseback. Most people in this tradition fall back on whatever is closest to hand on the day of need.

The great merit of this wing of evangelicalism is that it approaches scripture as a means of grace. Its focus is on personal conversion, the quest for sanctification, and the fullness of the life of the Spirit here and now. Its goal is the renewal of the church as much as its reform. The driving force is salvation — real, intimate, personal knowledge and encounter with the living God here and now as a foretaste of the life to come. Hence the core of the tradition is not epistemology but soteriology. Doctrines of inerrancy and infallibility are displaced from prominence by doctrines of justification, regeneration, assurance, and sanctification.

I am displaying my own Methodist and Wesleyan heritage in the moves that I am making here. For Wesley, salvation included not just justification but sanctification. He had a complex, and sometimes not altogether healthy, doctrine of sanctification. Scripture's primary function is to make us wise unto salvation. Within this trajectory, the seeker or believer pores over scripture as a way of coming to meet God in the heart, as a journey of love leading to the appropriation of the mind of Christ, as a means of attaining a knowledge of God that is through scripture but above and beyond scripture.

To put the matter this way is to court suspicion within certain segments of evangelicalism.

At one level, epistemology has been relativized. The concern is less knowing how we know about God than knowing God. Even while the captivity of scripture to epistemology remains, epistemology is often idling or sidelined. Hence, while there may well be a theory of inspiration or revelation hovering in the background, there is room to take it or leave it; or, better, to readjust it and enrich it.

At a second level, there is a tendency here and there to develop epistemological insights whose implications may be explosive. The best example of this is the appeal to the witness of the Spirit or the experience of God. They constantly threaten to undermine the appeal to scripture or divine revelation. Alternatively, properly thought through, these insights can enrich the epistemology of theology. (On some of this, Wesley was actually pretty good.) There are epistemological insights that people don't quite know what to do with. You can go one way or another with them, but they are there in the bosom of the tradition.

At a third level, there is a recurring effort to reach back to material outside scripture and place it alongside scripture. The most notable example is the appeal to the classical creeds of the church in the patristic period. To be sure, efforts will be made to trace these back to scripture, but this is more a bow to the background theory than it is a serious enterprise. Much more is going into the development of the doctrine of the Trinity than simply reading Bible verses.

All of these moves are conspicuously visible in the tangled and somewhat amateurish theology of John Wesley.

Wesley's heart and soul were taken up with soteriology. His epistemology and doctrine of scripture, like his doctrine of the Trinity, were frankly ad hoc and second-hand. He was, at times, committed to a doctrine of divine dictation, as were many other evangelicals prior to the nineteenth century. His treatment of inspiration was crude and abrupt. He was perfectly happy to let Matthew copy errors from his sources. Generally, John Wesley was more a medieval than a modern figure. Like Thomas Hooker, the great Anglican, and Aquinas, he believed that if we have access to divine revelation, that settles the issue. Arguments from tradition, reason, and experience were essentially apologetic strategies to bring recalcitrant opponents on board. This represents a radically different way of handling what is called the Wesleyan Quadrilateral than has been the case, for example, in the hands of Albert Outler.

Wesley came alive when he turned to soteriology. He was captivated by the doctrine of the Christian life, as we can see from his standard sermons. They were organized around a threefold scheme. Phase one is becoming a Christian — getting clear access to justification, regeneration, and assurance. Phase two is going on to a perfection made visible by the content of the Sermon on the Mount. Phrase three is Christian paranesis — spiritual and prudential advice for coping with the vicissitudes of daily living after one has gone through phases one and two. Epistemology has been supplanted by soteriology.

Yet Wesley did not entirely abandon epistemology. He mined the doctrine of the inner witness of the Holy Spirit for all it was worth. In doing so, he relocated the doctrine where it belongs. The witness of the Spirit is not, as Calvin and others made it, an epistemic device to secure the identity of the true canon. It is part of the doctrine of Christian assurance where one comes to know the love of God for oneself, crying out "Abba, Father" as one responds in faith to the gospel. As such, it is a form of perception of the divine.

Here Wesley was reaching back into the ancient tradition of the spiritual census in which the pure in heart see God for themselves. Perhaps it is no accident that William Alston, reared two centuries later within Methodism and in the shadow of Wesley, should have latched onto the perception of the divine as the key to the epistemology of Christian belief. It is certainly no accident that Methodists took to liberal Protestantism in the late nineteenth century in Boston as the proverbial duck takes to water.

Finally, Wesley was at pains to put scripture in a wider tapestry of spiritual practices, materials, and persons. While he knew that his sermon on the Trinity was inadequate, he also knew that his brother's hymns had captured the heart of the matter. In his quest for valid ordinations, he made a mess of the practice of episcopacy. But his very practice displayed the intuition that oversight is a charismatic and canonical phenomenon essential to the welfare of the church. He had a high view of the sacraments. He selectively loved the patristic teachers of the church. Like his love feasts, his General Rules were a remarkable experiment in recovering the spiritual practices of the church, with accountability built in. In forming the church in America, he clearly saw the importance of providing an agreed form of liturgy. In short, Wesley tried valiantly to retrieve and redeploy much of the wider canonical heritage of the patristic tradition, albeit expressed in the conventions of a later time and place.

Perhaps the most interesting point to note is that, in editing the Articles of Religion and sending them to his followers in North America, Wesley retained the modest soteriological doctrine of scripture as he found it in Anglicanism, rather than substituting his own more epistemologically oriented proposals. In short, Wesley at his best came back to scripture as a means of grace, holding at bay the constant temptation to reach for some form of classical foundationalism as the heartbeat of his doctrine of scripture.

In this, of course, he is not alone. Wesley is simply one person in a network of movements, associations, and fellowships that have been the core of evangelicalism in the wider church and popular culture. In many and varied ways, they have sought to keep scripture alive as a means of grace. As in the field of epistemology, much remains to be done. We need a richer account of the full canonical heritage of the church. We need a more delicate account of how the Holy Spirit uses this to bring us to Jesus Christ and to perfect us in love. And we need a fitting analysis that relates all this to epistemology without our falling prey to philosophy.

Evangelicals across the centuries have operated in a world held captive to the primacy of epistemology. Within this world they have creatively engaged the epistemological issues that swirl around scripture, and they have kept alive an older and healthier conception of scripture as a means of grace.

This is neither a battered old Ford, nor is it a new Cadillac. It is a solid, reliable Toyota. Not everyone will want to buy it, but it is road worthy. At the very least, it deserves to be test-driven in the contemporary academy.

# Trinitarian Theology

## ALISTER McGRATH

L et me begin with a note about evangelicalism in Europe.
There is something of a difference between British and
North American evangelicalism. As Mark Noll made clear, evangelicalism, particularly in England, has tended to be a trend inside the
mainline denominations, particularly, of course, the Church of England. We find similar patterns in Scotland, Denmark, Sweden,
Finland, and other parts of Europe, and this gives a significantly
different aspect to European evangelicalism. There is a strong
sense of a family history, a sense that evangelicalism did not begin
this century or last century, but that it goes back to the evangelical
revivals of the eighteenth century, to the European Reformation of
the sixteenth century, and even beyond that to the patristic heritage itself. There is a sense of belonging, of being rooted in history,
of doing what James Packer calls "great-tradition Christianity." In
North America, many evangelicals choose to become Greek Orthodox, feeling there is a strong sense of history in that tradition that
is lacking in evangelicalism. In European evangelicalism, because
of its strong sense of being rooted in history, that trend simply isn't
present to anything like the same extent.

Trinitarian theology is a very generous theme. I want first to say something about the importance of theology itself, because over the last twenty years, evangelicalism has become more theologically sophisticated and committed. This demonstrates a new confidence, a new willingness to engage with the issues on the agenda of the academy. I have been saddened by people who begin their Christian lives as evangelicals but then decide to leave the movement, feeling that it lacks intellectual grounding and sophistication, and so we lose them. The new emphasis on theology can be helpful in encouraging us to discover — not to invent, but to discover — the richness in the evangelical tradition.

Perhaps there are also disadvantages to this rediscovery. Theology creates controversy. And then there is the more serious difficulty that the heartbeat of evangelicalism is Christ-centered piety — a sense of wonder and excitement that there is something here that is profoundly worth having and that relativizes and overshadows everything. This leads to worship, adoration, and the writing of hymns rather than theological textbooks. Perhaps evangelicalism tends to express its theology more in praise and prayer than in theological reflection.

Most evangelicals do not talk about the Trinity at all. I have read some seven books by John Stott, the noted British evangelical, looking for specific references to the Trinity. They are few, and they occur in three different contexts: (1) The Trinity undergirds the authority of scripture. The Bible is the witness of the Father to the Son through the Holy Spirit. (2) The Trinity undergirds the centrality of Jesus Christ by providing intellectual justification for this Christ-centered focus. (3) The Trinity makes evangelism difficult in relation to adherents of Judaism and Islam, who naturally think that Christians are tritheistic. There is no sense, at least in Stott, that the Trinity is the cornerstone of evangelical identity.

Why is that? One of the reasons is that evangelicalism, deep down, is actually quite populist. It is very concerned about ordinary Christian believers rather than theologians. I note that and do not criticize it, because in many ways the reason evangelicalism is growing is not because its experts produce theological tomes, but because it proves capable of relating to ordinary people, of speaking their language, of engaging with them, of offering them a vision that changes their lives and focuses on the very simple Christ-centered piety. Often the Trinity is seen as implicit in but not at the forefront of what is believed about Jesus. The real heartbeat of evangelicalism is in a church Bible study group. If you go there and listen, there will be a lot about Jesus and Jesus' impact on us. But the Trinity is not seen as centrally important; it is seen as difficult.

One of my most forceful childhood memories from rural Ireland is of being in a country church when I was about thirteen. We were saying the Athanasian Creed, and we droned on: "There is the Father, incomprehensible; there is the Son, incomprehensible; there is the Holy Ghost, incomprehensible." A farmer beside me said, far too loudly, "The whole damn thing is incomprehensible!" You can see what he meant.

Evangelicalism has a passionate commitment to Jesus Christ, and the Trinity may well be implicit in this. It may be that thinking about the Trinity reinforces and undergirds our commitment to Christ, but the Trinity is not seen as being of major importance.

It is important to realize nevertheless that evangelicalism is trinitarian and that this is something to be welcomed and cherished. Evangelicalism is perhaps best seen as traditional, orthodox Christianity with certain very definite emphases: on conversion, for example, on the authority of Scripture, on the centrality of Christ's redemptive work on the Cross. One could argue that these beliefs are the common heritage of the Christian tradition, but for evangelicals they are where the emphasis is placed. To emphasize certain beliefs does not mean abandoning others. It simply means that these are of central importance, but there are others as well.

We need to unpack evangelicalism's heritage and realize that the doctrine of the Trinity does offer important insights for the evangelical tradition as it forges ahead. The doctrine of the Trinity, to put it simply, reminds us that there is far more to God than any of us can grasp. There is a tendency within sections of evangelicalism, for entirely understandable reasons, to focus on one of the persons of the Trinity. At a very simplistic level, one might say that a Christ-centered piety focuses on the second person, and a more charismatic approach focuses on the third person of the Trinity. Nevertheless, these are different emphases within a common tradition. Charismatics and evangelicals belong to the same group. They may place the stress in different places, but nonetheless a commonality exists between them.

Trinitarian theology allows us to begin to rediscover that evangelicals do believe in God the creator. We have placed the emphasis — and rightly so — on the wonderful work of redemption accomplished in Christ that changes our lives and gives us hope, purpose, and something to say to people. But alongside that there is a belief that this God who redeems is also a God who created. We need to rediscover the importance of the doctrine of creation in relation to our ecological crisis — the insight that this is not our world; it was made by God and has been entrusted to us, but it is not ours. It is God's, and we are responsible to God for what we do with it.

Evangelicals have also neglected natural theology and engagement with the natural sciences, both of which were central to the evangelical heritage in the seventeenth century. The doctrine of creation allows us to recapture the tradition of going to the creation and learning more about the Creator. The two books — the book of nature and the book of scripture — complement each other in a most wonderful way. Natural theology is the basis for apologetics, and rediscovering the Trinity is very important for this agenda.

Tom Smail, a British author, wrote a book called *The Forgotten Father*. The title means that evangelicals tend to focus on either Christ or the Spirit but say surprisingly little about God the Father. Perhaps there is something we can do about that.

We need to see the relationship between classical evangelicalism and the charismatic movement, or between perhaps "word-centered" and "spirit-centered" evangelicalism. Moreover, they can learn from and complement each other. There is always a danger that the charismatic movement will become so experiential that it has no contact with the world of thought, no contact with scripture, no contact with Jesus Christ. And there is a danger that a more word-centered theology may simply be "right thoughts" about Jesus, lacking the real experiential dimension that was so important to Wesley before us and that has reemerged as important in our own day.

A trinitarian perspective allows us to bring these strands together to mutually enrich one another and say that there is no need to drive a wedge between a richly Christ-centered spirituality and a spirituality that stresses experience. The doctrine of the Trinity begins to allow us to see how we can give intellectual justification to that kind of approach. The Trinity may not be of central importance to evangelicals at the grassroots level, but the insights it articulates are of fundamental importance to evangelicals as we move ahead and face the future.

Theology gives us an idea of what God is like. It so moves us that our minds and hearts are going to be restless until we have encountered and engaged this God to whom theology points. The doctrine of the Trinity challenges us to ask whether we have limited God; whether we have fully grasped God in all of God's fullness; whether our worship and theology do justice to this wonderful God who has created and redeemed us and who sustains us now. Theology is about building a vision of who God is, a vision that forces us to our knees as we recognize that we are in the presence of something that excites us and makes us want to do something. A Trinitarian theology paints before our eyes the full richness of who this God of the Christians is and why we need to respond to this God — in obedience, in prayer, and in theological reflection. There is always a tendency to fail to appreciate God for all that God is. The doctrine of the Trinity begins to put before our eyes a vision of the way that God actually is, so that we become excited about what we find.

Evangelicalism is passionately in love with this living God who has come to us in Christ, who demands that we respond not simply with our minds but with our hearts and lives and say, "Here is something worth giving up everything." It is "the pearl of great price" that so transcends everything else that it is worth selling all in order to possess it. The doctrine of the Trinity paints a picture of this God and asks to get down on our knees as we realize how vast and wonderful God is.

Let me cite from a classic Reformed catechism that sets for modern evangelicalism a challenging agenda: "What," asks the Shorter Westminster Catechism, "is the chief end of Man?" The reply is short and simple, and it is a jewel in the theological crown of evangelicalism: "To glorify God and enjoy him forever." How do we glorify this God? How do we enjoy this God? By understanding how amazing this God is. For evangelicals, one of the functions of the doctrine of the Trinity is to depict this God, to give us a vision and render us dissatisfied — not with who God is, but with our apprehension of God. And we will go away unsatisfied until we have accommodated our thoughts and lives to the way this God actually is. There is the sense that to glorify God, to enjoy God, we need to sweep to one side the limitations we impose on that God and encounter God as God really is.

Evangelicalism has been a missionary movement because it has seen in that message of a loving and redeeming God something that is worth taking to the ends of the earth. For evangelicalism, the great vision is of the prophet in Isaiah 6 going into the presence of the glory of God, realizing his sinfulness, and being purged of his sin, and then the question and answer, "Whom shall I send?" "Send me." There is a sense of a vision of God in all of God's glory leading to the desire to go out and talk about this wonderful God and all that God means. The doctrine of the Trinity is an affirmation of the wonder of God and a demand to us whether we have fully apprehended and responded to this God.

Saint Patrick, as far as we know, did not think of himself as an evangelical. But he bequeathed us insights we need to heed. I was born in Northern Ireland and baptized in 1953 in the cathedral of Downpatrick, the final resting place of the patron saint of Ireland. In the hymn "St. Patrick's Breastplate," Patrick (or his compiler) sets out a rigorously trinitarian approach to the Christian life. He surveys the panorama of the actions of God in order to bind that God to himself and go out to face the world and all its challenges.

The doctrine of the Trinity reminds us of the wonder of that God:

> I bind unto myself today
> The strong name of the Trinity

By invocation of the same,
The Three in One and One in Three.

As Patrick thinks about God the Creator, the hymn moves
on to survey the vast panorama of the works of God in history.
We are reminded that this God whom we have made our own
through faith is the same God who brought the earth into being.
As we contemplate the wonders of nature, we may grasp the astonishing insight that the God whose presence and power under-
gird the world of nature is the same God whose presence and
power are channeled into our individual existences. The believer
is constantly put in mind of the richness and depth of the Christian understanding of God, who has been bonded to the believer
through faith:

I bind unto myself today
The virtues of a starlit heaven,
The glorious sun's lifegiving ray,
The whiteness of the moon at even,
The flashing of the lightning free,
The whirling wind's tempestuous shocks,
The stable earth, the deep salt sea,
Around the old eternal rocks.

All of that — the incomparable vastness of the Creation — is
the God we are talking about. Then Patrick moves on to speak
about that same God in the great panorama of redemption:

I bind this day to me forever
By power of faith, Christ's incarnation;
His baptism in the Jordan River;
His cross of death for my salvation;
His bursting from the spicèd tomb;

His riding up the heav'nly way;
His coming at the day of doom;
I bind unto myself today.

Finally, this strong presence, this God is with us, sustains us, protects us, supports us:

I bind unto myself today
The pow'r of God to hold and lead,
His eye to watch, his might to stay,
His ear to hearken to my need,
The wisdom of my God to teach,
His hand to guide, his shield to ward,
The Word of God to give me speech,
His heav'nly host to be my guard.

And all that is true.

As we look around God's creation, as we contemplate all that Christ has done for us (that great evangelical emphasis), as we recollect that the same God sustains us even in life's darkest hours, we are talking about one and the same God doing all those things. It was St. Thomas Aquinas who reminded us that theology leads not so much to understanding but to adoration. We need to recall that, in the end, perhaps it is worship at which evangelicalism is its most authentic. As evangelicals contemplate all that God has done, the most authentic response is adoring God for what God is and what God has done.

We have a sense of dissatisfaction not with who God is, nor with the gospel, but with our grasp of this God, with our intellectual apprehension and the response we make to God. Recol-

lecting (in its dual sense of remembering and picking up) the doctrine of the Trinity, in effect, allows evangelicalism to open its
treasure chest, hold up its contents one by one, savor them, and
realize that there are enormous riches there — riches that have
been entrusted to us, that are there to sustain us in our mission
and ministry. One of those is the doctrine of the Trinity. It may be
difficult to understand, as that Irish farmer reciting the Athanasian Creed reminds us. But we are talking about something that,
in the end, leads not to understanding but to a sense of wonder
and amazement. There is something here that surpasses and
transcends everything we have known and that makes us want to
love and serve God.

That vision is still present in evangelicalism, and I hope it
will sustain us in whatever lies ahead.

# Disciplined Spirituality

## CHERYL SANDERS

My task is to define and describe disciplined spirituality as a characteristic feature of evangelical Christianity and to explore its significance for the faith of the church and the well-being of society. In keeping with our interest in evangelicalism at its best, I will assess a few representative expressions of disciplined spirituality from the vantage point of some of the best intersections evangelical faith has afforded white and black religion in America.

First some biographical background to this task. My doctoral dissertation in 1985 was a social and ethical analysis of the religious testimonies of African-American Christians who had been slaves. In most of my books since then, I have given attention to the worship, work, and witness of the Holiness and Pentecostal tradition and have shown a more general interest in how white and black Christians in the United States historically have engaged the claims of the gospel of Jesus Christ. For the past fourteen years, I have taught courses in Christian ethics, spirituality, and African-American religion and culture at a nondenominational, predominantly African-American, university-related theological school where the majority of students minister in Baptist, Methodist, and other mainline Protestant churches.

My own religious tradition is the Church of God (Anderson, Indiana), an interracial body of Holiness congregations. In 1997, I became senior pastor of the Third Street Church of God in Washington, D.C. I was saved, baptized, and grew up in this church, and my two children represent the fourth generation of my family's active participation there. I have served in various capacities over the years, including associate pastor for leadership development, minister of Christian education, Sunday School teacher, coordinator of youth ministries, and church historian. I have sought to continue and expand our congregation's emphasis on reconciliation and urban outreach, following the lead of the late Dr. Samuel George Hines, pastor of the church from 1969 to 1995.

The centerpiece of our ministry of reconciliation is the urban prayer breakfast, where 150 or more persons from the streets and homeless shelters of Washington gather each weekday morning for worship, preaching, prayer, Bible study, and a hot meal. I described this program and its philosophy in detail in my book *Saints in Exile: The Holiness-Pentecostal Experience in African-American Religion and Culture* (Oxford University Press, 1996), and also in my eighty-year history of Third Street Church, *How Firm a Foundation*.

I would define spirituality as the composite of invocation of and response to the divine presence. Evangelical spirituality frames these modes of engagement with the divine in terms of preaching and hearing the gospel of Jesus Christ. It is evangelical because it is centered on the announcement of good news.

Several spiritual disciplines are characteristic of (but by no means exclusive to) evangelical Christianity. They are preaching, prayer, praise, testimony, and Bible study. Preaching comes first on my list not because of any clerical hegemony, but because evangelical spirituality is grounded in personal response to the preaching of the gospel of Jesus Christ and the inherent invitation to Christian discipleship.

The key to understanding the connection between preaching and spirituality is found in Paul's letter to the Romans:

> For whosoever shall call upon the name of the Lord shall be saved. How then shall they call on him in whom they have not believed? And how shall they believe in him of whom they have not heard? And how shall they hear without a preacher? And how shall they preach, except they be sent? As it is written, "How beautiful are the feet of them that preach the gospel of peace, and bring glad tidings and good things!" But they have not all obeyed the gospel. For Isaiah saith, "Lord, who hath believed our report?" So then faith cometh by hearing, and hearing by the word of God. (Romans 10:13-17)

Evangelicals uniformly relate preaching and hearing the gospel to the imperatives of the great commission (Matthew 28:19), where Jesus directs his disciples to teach and baptize persons of all nations, although it doesn't exactly say "preach to them."

Prayer is the second spiritual discipline that is indispensable to evangelical faith. Prayer is conversation with God that, at its best, entails petition and reflection, thanksgiving and complaint. Prayer is always included in corporate worship and is encouraged as a vital component of the day-to-day living of individuals and families. The National Prayer Breakfast is one example of the strength and diversity of evangelical public piety. This event draws an international company of evangelicals each year to a hotel ballroom in Washington, in the company of the president, members of the Cabinet and Congress, celebrities, professional athletes, and religious leaders.

The various liturgies of the evangelical churches all place great emphasis upon praise and adoration of Jesus. In particular, it is the hymnody of evangelical Christianity that marks the distinctive character of praise and most expressly conveys its theological intent and commitments. Many of these songs have been embraced by African-American churches, forming a common ground of confession apart from creeds and doctrine. They have broad appeal across denominations, races, and cultures:

> Amazing Grace, how sweet the sound,
> that saved a wretch like me.
> I once was lost, but now I'm found,
> was blind, but now I see.

> Blessed assurance, Jesus is mine!
> O, what a foretaste of glory divine!
> Heir of salvation, purchase of God,
> born of his Spirit, washed in his blood.
> This is my story, this is my song,
> praising my Savior all the day long.

> Because He lives, I can face tomorrow.
> Because He lives, all fear is gone.
> Because I know He holds the future,
> and life is worth the living just because He lives.

Testimony is the spiritual discipline of sharing one's faith in word and deed. The central feature of evangelical testimony is that one has known the Lord, or met the Lord, or accepted Christ as personal Savior, resulting in a transformed life of deep commitment and righteous endeavor. Although the evangelical emphasis upon behavioral "do's" and "don't's" is largely a thing of the past, there remains a significant correlation between one's confession of faith in Jesus Christ and adherence to some understanding of what constitutes a Christian lifestyle.

Bible study is a central spiritual discipline in evangelicalism. In evangelical churches, preaching tends to be expository. Sunday school is almost universal, and religious education generally is biblically based. Individuals are encouraged to read their Bibles regularly, and most of the aids to personal and group Bible study offered in bookstores are the products of evangelical minds and publishers. Evangelicals have been forthright and aggressive about developing computer software and Internet Web pages as resources for Bible study. Not to be overlooked is the fact that many of the best and most comprehensive biblical reference works, including commentaries, concordances, and dictionaries, are produced by evangelical scholars for use by pastors and lay people in the churches.

I must confess that one of my initial reactions to the invitation to address the topic of disciplined spirituality was to ask myself whether there was a not-so-subtle insinuation that if disciplined spirituality represents evangelicalism at its best, then somewhere out there is an undisciplined spirituality representing evangelicalism at its worst. Throughout the history of religion in America, and especially in view of various revivals and awakenings that engendered evangelical Christianity as we know it today, thoughtful observers have expressed grave doubts concerning overt manifestations of spirit in public worship. Some preachers and sociologists have reduced these allegedly inferior varieties of religious experience to so much noise and emotion.

Shall we assume that the term "disciplined" conveys some notion of strict decorum or orderly demeanor and adherence to Paul's dictum to the charismatic Corinthians to "let all things be done decently and in order" (1 Corinthians 14:40)? Or should discipline be differently understood as some sort of focused attentiveness to the broader dimensions and imperatives of Christian faith — the framework of action and reflection suggested by Jesus' advice to the lawyer (Luke 10:25-37), for example, that loving fidelity toward God and neighbor also implies a willingness to be inconvenienced by needy neighbors of other races and cultures? How shall we read the prophetic asceticism of John the Baptist, the holy boldness of Peter, the provocative preaching of Paul — as indicative of disciplined or undisciplined spirituality?

The best disciplined spirituality that evangelicals have to offer the church and society is the affirmation that the gospel of Jesus Christ fully entails both personal and social transformation. In this light, the operative understanding of "disciplined" is the consistent witness and work of the disciple. At the other extreme, undisciplined spirituality at its worst among evangelicals means loving or worshiping Jesus with no ear to the cries of the oppressed or the call to justice. Here the operative term is "decorum," achieved by silencing all who cry out, whether in praise or in pain.

I will try to illustrate the broader implications of disciplined and undisciplined spirituality with reference to three examples drawn from *God's Long Summer: Stories of Faith and Civil Rights* (Princeton University Press, 1997), a book by my fellow Harvard Divinity School alumnus, Charles Marsh. Marsh recounts the height of the civil rights struggle in Mississippi in the 1960s through the words and experiences of five persons who confessed Christian faith and who played divergent roles in the unfolding of events that culminated in the deaths of three civil rights workers — Michael Schwerner, James Chaney, and Andrew Goodman.

The first example is the First Baptist Church of Jackson, Mississippi. This massive congregation took up an entire city block near the state capitol building and was, according to Marsh, the single most powerful religious institution in Mississippi during the civil rights years. On a Sunday in June 1963, a group of students from Tougaloo College, a private black school, attempted to worship at First Baptist. One week later, the lay leadership of the church proposed a resolution, eventually adopted unanimously by the congregation, that lamented the current social unrest between whites and blacks yet called for First Baptist to limit its services to whites only. Marsh notes that the last black members of the church, who were former slaves, had been kicked out in 1868 as white Southerners responded in fear of black enfranchisement during Reconstruction. Later the church's in-house historian justified this move by noting the difference in black and white styles of worship and "the need to preserve the solemn eloquence of white religion." Marsh concludes that the singing and praying of the church visitors on the front steps almost a century later met with equal disapproval.[1] Here the "solemn eloquence of white religion" enabled a total bifurcation of spirituality and social responsibility and a missed opportunity to be enriched by interracial worship and dialogue.

The second example comes from another prominent evangelical congregation in Jackson, the Galloway Memorial Methodist Church. Like First Baptist, Galloway had enacted a policy of excluding worshipers based on race. Yet a white physics professor at Tougaloo College, John Garner, and his wife, Margrit, had been among a few members of Galloway who actively encouraged the clergy and laity to reconsider the church's closed-door policy. Marsh recounts how in the fall of 1963 Garner invited one of his students, Joyce Ladner, now president of Howard University, and two white out-of-state Methodist ministers to be his guests at Sunday school. Once they were in Garner's Sunday school class, several policemen entered the room and made arrests. Marsh describes the scene:

> The two ministers tried to explain to the policemen that they could not arrest Methodist clergy inside a Methodist church, but denominational polity was lost on Jackson's finest. The

1. Charles Marsh, *God's Long Summer* (Princeton: Princeton University Press, 1997), p. 101.

ministers asked the mortified church members to find Rever-
end Cunningham [the pastor] and bring him to the scene at
once, but Cunningham never appeared. John Garner then began calling on his fellow churchmen in the room by name, asking each one to inform the police of the absurdity of the arrest:
he was a member of this church! But his classmates remained
silent except for one woman who looked on the scene and began crying — whether with shame or sadness, Garner never
knew — and then covered her face with her hands and ran
down the hall out of sight. The police led the integrated group
out of the church into the police wagons and into city jail.
Along with his guests Garner was arrested for trespassing and
disturbing public worship. Although many people had certainly been arrested for praying or worshiping God in prohib-
ited places, no one in the civil rights movement (or perhaps in
the history of the Christian church) had ever been arrested for
the crime of attending his own church.[2]

Again, a morally bankrupt silence enables the Sunday
school class to resume its lessons after the undesirable member
and his guests are dragged away from the church by the police.

I cite the final example illustrating disciplined spirituality at
its best as manifested in the same racial struggle in Mississippi in
the mid-1960s, but this time with a courageous willingness to
speak and act truthfully in light of the word of God toward the
end of personal and social transformation. Fannie Lou Hamer
was a grassroots civil rights organizer from rural Mississippi who
came to national prominence during her outspoken leadership of
the Mississippi Freedom Democratic Party at the 1964 Democratic National Convention in Atlantic City. The previous summer, she had been arrested along with a group demanding to be

2. Marsh, *God's Long Summer,* p. 139.

served at a segregated lunch counter. She was brutally beaten at the county jail in Winona, Mississippi.

Marsh recounts Mrs. Hamer's beating as a kind of Golgotha. Her torture might well have ended in death had not an unidentified white man stopped the beating. Mrs. Hamer was certain that death was imminent. There was no singing that night. Yet the next day her despair was transformed and song broke free. She sang:

> Paul and Silas was bound in jail, let my people go.
> Had no money for to go their bail, let my people go.
> Paul and Silas began to shout, let my people go.
> Jail doors opened and they walked out, let my people go.[3]

Marsh summarizes Fannie Lou Hamer's relationship with her tormentors:

> Later, when Mrs. Hamer was escorted by the jailer himself to her trial, she put the question to the very man who had helped carry out her beating just a few days earlier, "Do you people ever think or wonder how you'll feel when the time comes you'll have to meet God?" His response was full of embarrassment and vigorous denial. "Who you talking about?" he mumbled. In fact, Mrs. Hamer knew all too well what had happened. "I hit them with the truth, and it hurts them," she said.[4]

Marsh concludes that this terrifying experience brought her face to face with her worst fears about white racist violence, civil rights activism, and herself. Yet she was empowered by freedom songs and "the truth," and thus she emerged full of courage and

---

3. Marsh, *God's Long Summer*, p. 22.
4. Marsh, *God's Long Summer*, p. 23.

righteous anger: "She said, 'I am never sure anymore when I leave home whether I'll get back or not. Sometimes it seems like to tell the truth today is to run the risk of getting killed. But if I fall, I'll fall five feet four inches forward in the fight for freedom. I'm not backing off.'"[5]

Which evangelicals epitomize disciplined spirituality — those who sing and shout and speak out too loudly for the cause of justice, or those whose entire religious experience is governed by silent conformity to exclusive racial practices and relentless manifestations of cultural contempt?

At its best, disciplined spirituality evokes disciplined ethics: courage to confront even the most deeply entrenched evils of the society; wisdom to develop constructive alternatives and strategies to rectify past injustices and promote a just future; and compassion to bring about reconciliation and human wholeness wherever possible.

5. Marsh, *God's Long Summer,* p. 24.

# Evangelical Ethics

## RICHARD MOUW

The publication of Carl Henry's *Christian Personal Ethics* in 1957 was an important intellectual breakthrough for the North American evangelical movement. Scholarly ethical discussion by twentieth-century North American evangelical thinkers was a scarce commodity. Certainly nothing like Henry's hefty tome had appeared in this century. While Henry's book was an important step in the direction of filling a void, he intentionally chose to restrict the focus of his theological attention to "the sphere of personal ethics,"[1] with only occasional and rather minimal references to social and political questions.

For many of us who came to positions of evangelical leadership a decade or so later, with an ethical consciousness that was shaped by the mood of social activism in the 1960s, this restricted focus presented some problems of its own. For one thing, it meant that we still had almost no contemporary evangelical scholarly literature to turn to in our own attempts to address the

---

1. Carl F. H. Henry, *Christian Personal Ethics* (Grand Rapids: Eerdmans, 1957), p. 17.

most burning issues of the day, which tended to be more structural than systemic in nature.

Furthermore, many of us found it difficult to work with the received distinction between personal and social ethics. Needless to say, it wasn't only evangelicals like Henry who thought that these labels represented a natural division of labor in ethical thought. I once heard a mainline Protestant ethicist announce that, while evangelicals were exclusively concerned with personal issues such as gambling, profanity, and the use of alcohol, liberals like him were more interested in addressing such social matters as racism, sexism, and the environment. Many of us had come to see this as an arbitrary way of carving up the ethical terrain. Why is it a personal sin to take the Lord's name in vain, but a social offense to use masculine pronouns in purporting to refer to persons of both genders? Why is opposition to state lotteries a personal matter, while lobbying against environmental pollution is an instance of social action?

This was an issue that some of us, as evangelicals, devoted much thought to in the 1970s as we felt compelled to acknowledge more intimate links and overlaps between the personal and the social. But we also wanted to be careful not simply to eliminate or play down personal religion in favor of a social consciousness. As heirs to the variety of pietist and pietist-type movements of the past, all evangelicals strongly emphasize the need for an intensely personal, experiential appropriation of the claims of the gospel. From such a perspective, a proper recognition of the need for a social ethic can never be purchased at the expense of denying the importance of a deeply personal faith that is expressed in, among other things, a strong sense of moral seriousness about very personal relationships and practices. Clarifying those matters was an important project for many of us in the 1970s, and now evangelicals of a variety of political persuasions function as a very visible presence in the North American public arena.

I myself had a hard time finding evangelical sources in thinking about these things back in those days. When I turned to varieties of liberal Protestant Social Gospel thought, to some of the emerging Catholic liberation theology, and to some of the other traditions of radical social consciousness, I found nothing that spoke to my wholeness as both a personal and social entity. As I struggled with this as an evangelical, I finally found that evangelical hymns were really my best source. I found that I had learned the language of radical discipleship in the altar call and at the mourning bench.

Think of those hymns that we sang when every head was bowed, and every eye closed, and no one was looking around: "As you are all on the altar of sacrifice . . . I surrender all, I surrender all, I hold nothing back. . . . Have thine own way, Lord; have thine own way. Thou art the potter, I am the clay. Mold me and make me after Thy will, while I am waiting. . . ." That is the language of radical commitment.

Unfortunately, the evangelicalism that had nurtured many of us restricted the radical questions to such things as personal sexuality and personal stewardship. So many of us during the 1960s and 1970s began to ask: Why shouldn't we also ask whether our racism should be left at the mourning bench? Why shouldn't we take our militarism and consumerism and our ethnic and racial identities and pride? Why shouldn't we take our ideological commitments, whether on the right or the left, place them on the altar of sacrifice, and surrender them to the lordship of Jesus Christ?

It was in the hymns that I learned and appropriated the claims of radical discipleship. Clarifying all those things was an important project for many of us in the 1970s. I actually considered for a while the possibility of doing an entire evangelical social ethic based on nothing but hymns that were sung by George Beverly Shea. (I spoke once at an evangelical conference about

God's concern for the poor and the oppressed. We weren't advocating radical programs of governmental economic redistribution; we were just saying, "God has a heart for the poor." God's concern is for those on the margins. Somebody raised a hand and said, "You didn't get this from the gospel. You got this from Karl Marx." My response was, "No, I got it from George Beverly Shea.")

When I was seven years old, I got my first record player (one of the old wind-up types), and the very first record I was given was of George Beverly Shea's hymns. I was so fascinated with this new technology that I memorized all the hymns in the process of playing them over and over again. There was one that went something like this (I quoted it to the person who asked me the question about Marx): "I'd rather have Jesus than silver or gold, I'd rather have Jesus than riches untold. I'd rather have Jesus than houses or lands, I'd rather be true to his nail-pierced hands than to live. . . ."

Once you've learned that, Karl Marx is tame! If you can sing, "I'd rather have Jesus than silver or gold . . . than houses or lands," what are you going to do about the homeless? What are you going to do about a world in which there are millions of starving people and abused children? What are you going to do about that? It was in those radical calls to discipleship that many of us learned what social action is all about, and now the case for evangelical social action has been made.

In his Introduction to *Christian Personal Ethics,* Carl Henry called for evangelicals to formulate "a comprehensive revealed ethic, full-orbed as Christian theology."[2] But that is not likely to be the sort of product on which evangelical ethicists could ever achieve consensus. For all of our accolades to "sound theology," evangelicals do not really insist on common agreement to an all-encompassing, tightly defined system of thought. We are too much of a coalition embracing a variety of theological traditions

2. Henry, *Christian Personal Ethics,* p. 16.

(Reformed, Wesleyan, Pentecostal, dispensationalist, and so on) to be capable of achieving that kind of precision. Rather, we rally around a common set of corrective emphases in theology and spiritual practice.

Alister McGrath illustrated this feature nicely when he responded to the oft-stated charge that evangelicals have "an underdeveloped ecclesiology" by suggesting that maybe "it is others who have overdeveloped ecclesiologies."[3] Evangelicals have long worried about ecclesiological perspectives that are so highly detailed and all-consuming that they crowd out other important theological concerns. So we respond by emphasizing some things, such as the need for a personal relationship with Jesus Christ and for evangelizing the lost, that are often neglected by people who take delight in detailed ecclesiologies.

What is true of evangelical theology in general applies to ethics in particular. Evangelical ethical thought will, at its best, also function more as a set of corrective emphases than as a detailed moral theology. As I have already suggested, the most recent spurt of corrective activity has been largely directed toward remedying some of our own past evangelical ethical patterns, with a special focus on the spirit of separatism that has often placed a high premium on Christian withdrawal from public life. But we also continue to be aware of the need for evangelical correctives to what goes on in the broader Christian ethical discussions. Some of these very important correctives have to do with matters that would have been almost universally taken for granted in the Christian past but are widely ignored today in much ethical discussion, such as the insistence that there is a God who has issued clear directives for the moral life; that these

3. Alister McGrath, "Evangelical Anglicanism: A Contradiction in Terms?" in *Evangelical Anglicans: Their Role and Influence in the Church Today*, ed. R. T. France and A. E. McGrath (London: Society for Promoting Christian Knowledge, 1993), p. 14.

directives are presented to us in an authoritative scripture; and that we sinners are urgently in need of rather detailed divine ethical guidance since, if we are left to our own devices, we will inevitably be led astray by a human "heart [that] is deceitful above all things, and desperately wicked" (Jeremiah 17:9). Other corrective concerns arise out of the special ways in which pietist Christians have wrestled with rather fundamental questions about our relationships with the larger human community.

I will concentrate on these latter concerns. In doing so, I want to suggest that the time has come to reappropriate some of the theological themes that evangelical ethicists have played down for a while as we worked diligently to compensate for past insensitivities to systemic and structural matters. In this effort at reappropriation, it might be a good time to think about the ways in which we can honor, albeit in a "post-systemic" manner, the past evangelical fondness for Christian personal ethics.

On the one hand, I am interested in the relationship of the ethical concerns of evangelicalism to the evangelical community's actual social location — a connection whose importance Alasdair MacIntyre has highlighted in insisting (in defense of his well-known thesis that "[a] moral philosophy . . . characteristically presupposes a sociology") that we attend to "the correlation between an ethical system and its actual or possible patterns of collective embodiment."[4] The other relationship has to do with how evangelicalism's ethical concerns fit into the larger set of our theological convictions; the "mapping" of this larger framework is a necessary task, as Marilyn McCord Adams has cogently argued, if Christians are to have an adequate grasp of their understanding of "moral value and the human good."[5]

4. Alasdair MacIntyre, *After Virtue: A Study in Moral Theory* (Notre Dame: University of Notre Dame Press, 1981), p. 22.

5. Marilyn McCord Adams, "Problems of Evil: More Advice to Christian Philosophers," *Faith and Philosophy* 5 (April 1988): 139.

One of the less visible products of the recent surge of evangelical public activism is the significant number of younger evangelical professionals who have gained entry to jobs in the public arena in the past decade or so. If you want direct evidence at Harvard University, look at the strong group of evangelicals who have an organized presence in the Kennedy School of Government. A while back, I met with a group of about two dozen such individuals in Washington, D.C., most of them in their twenties and thirties. They were employed by congressional staffs, lobbying groups, federal agencies, and think tanks. I found them to be a very thoughtful group, intensely interested in integrating their basic evangelical convictions with the day-to-day pursuit of their work assignments. Most of them are involved in prayer-breakfast-type fellowships. But they have also formed some small groups specifically devoted to theological and ethical reflection. One of them reported, for example, that his group had recently devoted several weekly meetings to discussing the differences between John Howard Yoder's Anabaptist writings and the views of various Reformed thinkers.

As these young evangelicals talked about the theological issues that most concern them in their work in the public arena, three dominant questions emerged. First, how should we see our involvement in public life as flowing from our identity as members of the body of Christ? Second, to what degree can we expect success in our efforts to promote public righteousness during this time when we still await the return of Christ? And third, what is the proper mode of public discourse for Christians who are themselves immersed in the thickness of Christian convictions? (The words "thick" and "thin" come from Evans Pritchard, who got them from Gilbert Ryle. A thick description takes into account the highly detailed and nuanced values and beliefs of the person being described. A thin description is a broader, more neutral description.)

These questions fall within three important sub-disciplines of Christian thought: ecclesiology, eschatology, and epistemology (doctrine of the church, doctrine of last things, and theory of knowledge). Although none of the questions raised are completely foreign to persons in other Christian traditions and movements, there are distinctive ways in which evangelicals formulate the theological concerns that are at stake in dealing with those three questions.

At the risk of oversimplifying, I am going to put the case in rather simple terms. Evangelicals of the past have configured their thinking in these areas by weaving together three strands of thought: first, a remnant ecclesiology in which the true church is seen as a cognitive minority; second, an apocalyptic eschatology that understands the larger culture as heading toward destruction; and third, an antithetical epistemology that insists on a radical difference between Christian and non-Christian interpretations of reality. In some periods, these strands have been more dominant than at other times. But even when evangelicals replaced them with perspectives that were less negative in emphasis, they were never completely suppressed. They lurk in the corners of evangelical consciousness as mindsets that must always be reckoned with. The result is the presence of ongoing tensions in evangelical thought, and the tensions often are clearly at work in evangelical ethical wrestlings.

The role that these three strands have played in the not-so-distant past is nicely documented in Joel Carpenter's recent study of American fundamentalism in the 1930s and '40s.[6] But I will give a more personal version of the story. When I was growing up

6. Joel Carpenter, *Revive Us Again: The Reawakening of American Fundamentalism* (New York: Oxford University Press, 1997).

in the evangelical world, one of our favorite songs went like this: "This world is not my home, I'm just a-passing through. My treasures are laid up somewhere beyond the blue. The angels beckon me from heaven's open door, and I can't feel at home in this world anymore." We saw ourselves as a faithful band of believers in a world that was headed for destruction, which is to say that our otherworldliness was undergirded by a theological perspective in which the closely related themes of apocalyptic eschatology and remnant ecclesiology loomed large.

And we were also antitheticalists. We did not trust the ways in which non-Christian people, and especially non-Christian elites in the academy, set forth their views about the nature of reality and the good life. Non-Christian worldviews stood, in our reckoning, in a rather stark, antithetical relationship to what the Lord required of us. Evangelicalism's propensity for epistemological antitheticalism has been shaped in good part by pietism's very practical call (even to people who don't have the faintest idea what epistemological antitheticalism is) for Christians to shun all signs of worldliness, including a resistance to the thought patterns of this present evil age. When evangelicals have felt the need to provide a more technical theological rationale for this spiritual posture, they have often turned to Calvinism's strong emphasis on "the noetic effects of the Fall," drawing a stark contrast between regenerate and unregenerate cognition.

In North American evangelicalism, however, these strands have regularly stood in tension with other motifs — a fact that is spelled out nicely by Joel Carpenter in his analysis of what he labels, following George Marsden, some "paradoxical tensions" in the evangelical way of viewing our cultural presence. The negative strands are quite explicit when evangelicals are feeling marginalized by the larger culture. Then it is easy to see themselves as a remnant in a world headed for doom, thinking very different thoughts than anybody else. But evangelicals never really lose the deep hope that they might somehow rescue the culture itself. Revival is always at least a distant possibility lurking in our souls and the evangelical scheme. At the first hint of an opportunity to exercise cultural influence, the revivalist motif emerges and tends to become a formative influence in our thinking.

It seems obvious to me that this is what we have seen happen in the past few decades, as evangelical Christians, who not long ago viewed themselves as a cognitive minority, have been able to refer to themselves without embarrassment in recent years as "the moral majority," and have replaced the singing of "This world is not my home" with the very triumphalist "Shine, Jesus, shine, Fill this land with the Father's glory." Theologically, the shift can be seen in a number of phenomena. At Dallas Seminary, once a stronghold for the kind of dispensationalist theology in which remnant ecclesiology and apocalyptic eschatology loomed large, scholars now espouse a more muted form of what they call "progressive dispensationalism." That, too, is an important cultural phenomenon. Of special interest is the evidence of an epistemological shift in recent years. When traditional Calvinists have sensed a need to modify the more radical implications of their antitheticalist epistemology by exploring common ground between Christian and non-Christian thought, they have typically done so by introducing the notion of "common grace." This theme is now being regularly invoked in broader evangelical circles, accompanied by a strong interest in Roman Catholic natural law teachings.[7]

I must confess that there have been times in recent years when, given the ways in which some of these newer motifs have actually been employed by evangelicals in the public arena, I have

7. For the proceedings of a conference in which evangelicals and others discussed these themes, see Michael Cromartie, ed., *A Preserving Grace: Protestants, Catholics, and Natural Law* (Washington, D.C.: Ethics and Public Policy Center and Grand Rapids: Eerdmans, 1997).

secretly longed for the earlier days when we evangelicals saw ourselves as a remnant people, a cognitive minority content to live on
the margins of the culture. But in my better moments, I know
that a more appropriate response is one of ambivalence. The answer is not to retreat again into a separatist mode, but to move
more cautiously into the public arena while submitting to the
discipline of careful evangelical reflection, including reflection
on the positive lessons to be learned from the times of our past
marginalization.

There is some help to be gotten for this reflective task by
thinking critically about the views being put forth these days by
some non-evangelical scholars. Many of our own past evangelical
attitudes and moods have been taken up with a vengeance by
ethicists in other segments of the Christian community. An obvious example is found in that much-quoted concluding paragraph
of Alasdair MacIntyre's *After Virtue,* where he speaks in apocalyptic terms of "the new dark ages" in which we live, thus issuing his
call for local remnant communities who will sustain the moral
life as they wait "for another — doubtless very different — St. Ben-
edict."[8] It is also very easy to find variations on these remnant-
apocalyptical-antithetical motifs in the writings of Stanley
Hauerwas,[9] who has been very vocal in his insistence that Christian ethics must be grounded in the practices of a highly particu-
larized Christian community that sees its moral discourse as radically discontinuous with the larger culture.

While evangelicals should not uncritically embrace these
current blends of apocalyptic eschatology and remnant ecclesiology, neither should they simply dismiss them out of hand.
Here, too, ambivalence is an appropriate response. MacIntyre

8. MacIntyre, *After Virtue,* pp. 244-45.
9. See for example Stanley Hauerwas, *After Christendom? How the Church Is
to Behave If Freedom, Justice, and a Christian Nation Are Bad Ideas* (Nashville:
Abingdon Press, 1991).

and Hauerwas are providing important reminders to evangelicals of our older configuration of remnant-apocalyptic-antithetical convictions. The facts of contemporary life suggest that we need these reminders in our attempts to understand our present calling as Christians, even as we place those attempts into a larger context that has been filled out by more recent explorations of our place in the larger human community. The neo-apocalypticists may be right in their insistence that we are, indeed, living in a very bad day. But this is also, to borrow a Mennonite phrase that John Howard Yoder regularly put to good use, "the time of God's patience." And since God is presently tolerating some very bad human behavior, then it is quite proper for Christians to imitate the divine patience by cultivating a spirit of long-suffering in public life, taking the gift of existence in the present age as an opportunity to cooperate with others in working for the common good.

Not that it is easy to hold all of this together. To be patient, for example, is not simply to stop worrying about patterns of life that are clearly in violation of God's revealed standards of righteousness. But proper patience does rule out public behaviors that stem from a spirit of self-righteousness. The antithesis between godliness and ungodliness is very real; it is discernible, however, not only in the larger patterns of culture but also in the inner battlegrounds of our own souls. How we speak and act faithfully in the larger public realm while working out our own salvation with the requisite fear and trembling — this challenge is of supreme importance for evangelicals as we think about the proper rhythms of the life of discipleship.

Here the remnant ecclesiologies, both old and new, are helpful in the way in which they highlight the need for Christians to be immersed in the density of biblically grounded particularities. To be sure, it is also necessary — the urgings of remnantists, both old and new, to the contrary notwithstanding — for us to learn a thin public discourse that relies on the insights drawn from common grace and natural law perspectives. But our thin talk in the public arena can never be divorced from the thick convictions that guide our lives, both public and private. Indeed, it is precisely *in* the awareness of the particularities of our deepest convictions that we know the proper limits of our public discourse. The public arena as such can never rightly ban all thick expression, for it is also a forum where we give reasons for the hope within us. Thin discourse is most appropriate when we are talking with others about how best to structure our public lives as we draw the boundaries, together with those of other faiths and of no faith at all, that allow all of us to live out our deepest commitments with integrity.

It is a good thing, then, that evangelicals have been thinking and acting in recent decades in a manner that takes our public lives more seriously. The Christian gospel does call us to serve as witnesses to, and agents of, the reign of Christ in all spheres of human interaction. It is important for thick Christian communities to function, as Ronald Thiemann has put it, as "'schools of public virtue,' communities that seek to form the kind of character necessary for public life."[10] To be sure, our commitment to our own best understanding of what "public" is may on occasion be so out of line with the visions of public life being bandied about by our contemporaries that the most we can hope for is a holding action for the time being. As we look "for a city that has foundations" (Hebrews 11:10), it is enough for us to *await* the coming

10. Ronald Thiemann, *Constructing a Public Theology: The Church in a Pluralistic Culture* (Louisville: Westminster/John Knox Press, 1991), p. 43.

transformation by engaging in modest and civil efforts in the public arena as it is presently constituted, for we do anticipate something that is far better. All of this holds, even if the worst-case scenarios sketched out by the apocalypticists are accurate. Perhaps we are in the new dark ages. Perhaps a major cosmic conflict will soon come. Even so, we are obliged to seize the opportunities available to us as public agents during this time of God's patience.

How to accomplish all of that, of course, is not easy to discern. Even detailed visions of what constitutes a healthy public order will not do the whole job for us. We need very personal resources for living out our lives in the midst of the tragedy of existence as we presently experience it, both in our public and private interactions. Here I must confess that, for all of my deep loyalties to the Calvinist tradition, I find myself turning these days to other sources on some very basic issues. I find, for example, that John Calvin, who is well known for his emphasis on the ravages of sin in human affairs, often shows a surprising lack of sensitivity to the tragic dimensions of public life. Here (like Mark Noll, who has called for the addition of what he calls "the Lutheran leaven" to those theological systems like Calvinism that "encourage more straightforward and conclusive political thinking and more self-confidently direct political action")[11] I find Martin Luther to be a helpful guide. As Harro Hopfl has observed,[12] while Calvin fostered a systematic attention to the public-institutional ordering of life, Luther was far more interested in the character of the public leader and the spiritual manner of the Christian's involvement in the public arena. Luther's characterization of the calling of the Christian prince is especially poignant, and it can instruct us as a

11. Mark Noll, *Adding Cross to Crown: The Political Significance of Christ's Passion* (Grand Rapids: Baker Books, 1996), p. 35.

12. Harro Hopfl, ed., *Luther and Calvin on Secular Authority* (Cambridge: Cambridge University Press, 1991), pp. xiii-xiv.

more general word of advice for our callings as Christian citizens: the prince must be spiritually vigilant, Luther warns, if he wants to guarantee that "his condition will be outwardly and inwardly right, pleasing to God and men." In doing so, Luther quickly adds, the Prince "must anticipate a great deal of envy and suffering. As illustrious a man as this will soon feel the cross lying on his neck."[13]

On the issues of public life, Calvin was a more systematic thinker than Luther, and his views have therefore often had a high profile as Christians have thought about how best to shape political programs and movements. Luther's political reflections, on the other hand, are more in the genre of devotional reminders of the practical challenges and dangers of political life. Like all virtue-oriented accounts of the good life, it is easy to treat Luther's discussion as merely a helpful supplement to the more systematic treatments of the sort that Calvin offers. Perhaps this is legitimate. But in a contemporary climate where tragedy looms so large in the patterns of our corporate existence, and yet when evangelicals are, ironically, tempted by new moods of triumphalism, helpful supplements can sometimes provide us with our best sources of counsel. For that reason, we can hope that we will soon see some new, albeit "post-systemic" evangelical treatises on "Christian personal ethics."

Many Christians in the past have lived with a vivid sense of the tragic conditions under which they were called to serve the Lord. In a number of Christian traditions, it was common for believers to describe themselves, especially during periods of persecution and oppression, as members of "the churches under the cross." Perhaps it is time for evangelicals to revive that category of self-understanding, applying it this time in a spirit of humility to

13. Martin Luther, "On Secular Authority," in Hopfl, *Luther and Calvin on Secular Authority,* p. 41.

our broader responsibilities as citizens who work with others for the common good. This can be for us a new exercise in shunning worldliness, giving new meanings to our prayers that Jesus will keep us near the cross, as we seek the welfare of the cities in which we spend the time of our exile, yet ever watchful for the kind of large-scale renewal that can only be ushered in with the sound of heaven's trumpets.

# Living Tradition

## DAVID F. WELLS

W hat is the importance of tradition to evangelical faith, and what contribution might this make to academic culture today?

At first blush, tradition and evangelical faith seem like an improbable conjunction. It is not hard to find in the evangelical past many dismissive utterances about the Christian past. Indeed, this attitude hasn't only accompanied evangelical believing; it has often been the essence of it. From the Great Awakening to the present, American evangelicalism has had at its center the embrace of the ordinary person. It has been adept at knowing how to go along the highways and byways of life and find those very ordinary people. It has done so in the confidence that, when the truth is presented to them, they will be able to receive and accept it.

The less encumbered this truth is with references to the past and to academic speculations, the better everybody will be. As Nathan Hatch has helped us to see, the habits of our democracy have often become the habits of the evangelical impulse. The sovereignty of private decision-making is left to proceed without interruption from any complications like the Christian past.

87

There is another reason why this conjunction between tradition and evangelical theology seems improbable. For theological reasons, the word "tradition" doesn't have a very good ring in evangelical ears. What average people know about the Protestant Reformation may be quite minimal, but the one thing they seem to have been taught and to recall is that the Protestant Reformers opposed the word of God to tradition.

Much in the evangelical past replicates this antipathy. As it turns out, however, the Protestant reformers' view toward tradition was much more nuanced than this simple reading would suggest. One can, of course, find statements that are rather clear in their rejection of tradition and their belief that the Catholic Church arrogated to itself an authority it should not have. I quote Luther in a typical statement: "Our opponents skipped faith altogether and taught human traditions and works, not commanded by God but invented by them, without and against the Word of God. These they have not only put on a par with the Word of God, but they have raised these far above it." Yet it was Luther himself who contributed a little foreword to a book published in 1535 by an English churchman, Robert Barnes, called *Vitae Pontificum*. In the foreword Luther observed that, until this time, he had been opposing the papacy on the grounds of scripture. Now, he said, he was very happy to see that it could also be opposed on the grounds of history!

Until this time, the debate had been about where authority resided and what constituted the gospel. But now Luther began to see that the debate could also be put a little differently. Perhaps it was a contest between patristic and medieval Christianity, medieval having parted company with patristic by the addition of these accretions and traditions.

This line was developed perhaps more fully by the English Reformers. Thomas Cranmer, for example, said that where a consensus had emerged among the early Fathers, it should be seen as the fruit of the Holy Spirit's work. John Jewel observed that he would concede any point at all if there was clear patristic evidence to the contrary. Later, John Calvin, in his *Institutes*, would say: "If the contest were to be determined by patristic authority, the tide of victory, to put it very modestly, would turn to our side."

So began a debate that went on well into the next century over whether or not the Reformation could also be seen as a debate between patristic and medieval faith. It was a debate driven by polemical interests and sometimes skewered by those interests. While it is certainly the case that one can find people using history as a repository of opinions that could be raided in order to substantiate a doctrinal position they favored, it is also the case that there were those who came to see this history as a thing in itself — that the Holy Spirit who had inspired the scriptures had not then abandoned the church, but that there was in the life of the church a wisdom and an understanding that needed to be consulted and, where appropriate, assumed.

It is in this sense that evangelical theology, when it has acted on its best instincts, has self-consciously made itself a part of tradition. It is at its best when it has been able to bear within itself at least some of the wisdom, some of the understanding of Augustine and Calvin and Luther and Wesley and Edwards. The story, however, now becomes a little more complicated.

What contribution might a faith like this, informed and deepened by its connections with the past, make to academic culture today? The answer in practice entails another question: How will this stream of Christian thinking, which bears within itself as well as it can the wisdom of the past, encounter a modern consciousness that is so much a part of modern academic culture? And after the encounter, will it have anything left to say? This is a serious question, because we are really asking whether it is possible to make the transition from a premodern to a modern world.

When we look at Augustine and Luther, to take two of these representative figures, we are looking at people who lived in times that were markedly different from our own. The worlds they inhabited were made up of traditional societies that were essentially rural. We live in a time that is overwhelmingly urban. They lived in social hierarchies. We do not. In their worlds, the family was the most important social unit. It was the means by which values and understanding and knowledge were transmitted from generation to generation. In our world, the family doesn't have this centrality and often doesn't have this function at all.

In their societies, the sacred was matter-of-fact. In ours, it is not. For them, there were forms of traditional authority that, for us, have disappeared. It is true that we have authorities, but they are really part of our pluralism of expertise and don't function the way authorities once did. The bottom-line conclusion to all of this is that we, as moderns, are far more likely to be in perennial doubt, and to doubt far more things than these forebears in our Christian faith.

These differences are so fundamental to being modern that they have threatened to cut the lines of continuity from today back to the Christian past and, indeed, back to the New Testament. Rudolf Bultmann's well-known declaration that it is impossible for those who use electricity and modern technology to believe in the supernatural world of the Bible is a serious question. He went on to elaborate that worldviews are not simply garments that people can put on and take off at will; they are given to people in and with their social and cultural circumstances. We are inevitably and inescapably modern, since we are inescapably part of the modern context in which we live.

This debate over modern consciousness has been long and vexed and extremely complex. So what is modern consciousness, and how has it been constructed? There is something of a consensus that it is an amalgam, or perhaps the confluence of two streams. One has borne the ideas of the Enlightenment down to the present time; the other is a cultural stream. It is the cultural environment created by the processes of modernization — those processes that have so wrenched our world in the twentieth century and brought us more social change than anybody has ever seen before. The remarkable thing is that all of the social change has been accommodated almost silently, without most of the upheavals, civil wars, and social turmoil that accompanied just a fraction of social change like this in the past. At the confluence of these two streams, one intellectual and one cultural, modern consciousness was born, and these two realities have been in a symbiotic relationship.

On the one side, we have Enlightenment ideas about the nature and function of reason, the sovereignty of the knowing self, the necessity of tolerance, and the emancipation of our world from the presence, revelation, and providence of God. On the other side, there is the cultural context, the environment that has emerged from these processes of modernization. The modernizing process has given power and plausibility to the Enlightenment ideology. In combination, they have changed the way knowledge is organized, and they have authenticated a certain cognitive style that goes with being modern.

How does this work? Let me take the modernization side and pick up capitalism as one of the four major bearers of modernity. There is no doubt that the application of scientific rationality to the way that labor is organized and goods are produced has been remarkably effective. It has given us the most virile, abundant economic system that the world has ever seen. The atmosphere that accompanies it, however, is not value-neutral. Along with the abundance, we begin to notice the markers of modern consciousness almost hiding in it. For one thing, capitalism has brought about a reorganization that tends to sever public from private life, roughly corresponding to career and family. It tends, in its secularizing impulse, to strip public life of the reality of God, to marginalize him, to push him to the boundaries of what is relevant, and to strip the public square naked.

It tends to encourage people to function with different values in these different private and public contexts. This economic system that has been so abundant does not require everyone to be a hard-nosed materialist, but it certainly does promote that. It tends to socialize people into a kind of problem-solving mode, so that what is most efficient becomes what is ethically right. It therefore tends to exclude realms of knowing that once were considered very important to being human, but that today are considered irrelevant because they don't solve problems.

Take yet another part of modernization, that of urbanization. In this century we have become overwhelmingly urbanized, but what is the consequence of this? It is, of course, the loss of our communities. The consequence is that today people tend to be cut loose from place, certainly from community, and often from family. This is one of the factors, though not the only one, that have promoted an ideology of self-sufficiency and moral autonomy — the essence of the expressive individualism that sociologist Robert Bellah and others have worried about.

I have taken only two of what are generally agreed to be the four major bearers of modernity: urbanization, capitalism, technology, and means of mass communication. But together these feed off each other, reinforce each other, and produce a public environment that has, until relatively recently, made Enlightenment ideas seem so plausible and modern skepticism so normal. If it is so normal, is it also normative? Is it inevitable? Is it inescapable?

Bultmann certainly thought so, but I believe he was mistaken. It is certainly true that this modern context has a very subtle, coercive power, but it is not deterministic. This is why the older secularization thesis has proved wrong. Despite the fact that modernization has completely rearranged the landscape of America, religion has not vanished. Indeed, it is now flourishing. It is not clear to me either that those ideas are inevitable on the other side of this construction of modern consciousness — the Enlightenment ideology. In the postmodern world, we have seen them systematically challenged, one after another. In philosophy, there is a considerable attack being mounted on foundationalism — the idea that you have to have some indubitable beginning point for knowledge, which in turn seems to suppose that the mind is a mirror to reality. In the postmodern world, there are no foundations, only interpretations.

The same thing has happened with language. The discussion is very complex, but the end result is that a literary text is far less interesting than the subtext. We hear it in the postmodern attack on metadiscourse and metanarratives. The old Enlightenment idea that there was a goal, or a good, that was bigger than individual preference — whether this was the creation of wealth or a classless society — is under heavy assault today.

It is the case that the construction of knowledge in this postmodern world sets up an entirely different set of problems. It poses a world in which there is no objective or fixed or intelligible reality, a world in which we are all entirely contained within our own history. It is a history that is in flux, change, and movement. We no longer have the old objective world of the Enlightenment. What we have in its place is a set of chronic disagreements that seem to be entirely beyond resolution.

But I cite these instances of the postmodern attack upon the Enlightenment only to make this simple point: modern consciousness is not inevitable, and it is not deterministic. We will see in time, I am quite certain, that the postmodern consciousness wasn't any more enduring or normative either. As an evan-

DAVID F. WELLS

gelical, I like to go back in my mind, for example, to the vision in
the Book of Daniel in the Old Testament, in which he is shown
the civilizations coming and going. In the end, it is God alone
who endures. When I look at the modern world, I see something
like this going on. What Augustine believed, and what Martin Luther, Jonathan Edwards, or the Wesleys believed, was enduring because it was rooted in what God had revealed of himself. It was
not a product or an outcome of a particular set of circumstances.
While the issues raised in the postmodern and modern debates
are very important, they need to be taken with a kind of eternal
seriousness. This is a contribution that evangelical theology can
make to academic culture, because this theology has a way of
looking at reality that might not even occur to a modern or a
postmodern person.

How else might a theology rooted in Edwards, Augustine,
and company help us today? The representative figures that I
have mentioned were all, interestingly, church people. They spoke
from within it, they spoke to it, and they spoke for it. In so doing,
they remind us that theologians once had three audiences. In
America, in the Puritan scheme of things, it was initially the pastor who was the theologian. Theology was constructed in the
church and, more specifically, the pulpit. The church was its first
audience, but beyond that, society and the academy were also audiences.

The first audience to go was society, initially with the Revolution and the separation of church and state. Even more profoundly, the processes of modernization have given to our world a
temper that is disinterested in what theologians are talking about.
It is not that theologians cannot speak to the modern world; it is
just that they shouldn't be too disappointed if there isn't a large lis-
tening ear.

But what about the other two audiences, church and academy? With the emergence of seminaries at the beginning of the

94

last century, and divinity schools in the universities, the locus for doing theology shifted from the pulpit to the classroom. But then something else very important happened. By the end of the last century, like most fields of study, theology had become professionalized; theology, like any other field, was being mapped out. It had developed its own internal canons of credibility, its own style of discourse, its own literature, and its own experts who forwarded its interests and preserved its distinctiveness. Part of the preservation of theology, however, was often worked out in conjunction with the Enlightenment ideal of the neutrality and objectivity of reason. This meant that religious commitments were looked at askance. It also meant that in the academy, it became awkward to speak to the church. At the same time, the church appears to have accepted this divorce with some equanimity, perhaps less so in the mainline denominations and more so out in the evangelical hinterlands. Soon the practice of evangelical faith mercifully was released from the painful necessity of having to engage seriously with theological truth.

What might we look to in the future from an evangelical theology? First, with respect to its public role, it cannot co-opt society as a conversation partner, but it has a very important function and contribution to make. In any society like ours, three domains must be preserved: freedom, for it is the guardian of our creativity, our innovation, and our Christian believing; the law, because there are always law-breakers, and we need the full weight of the judicial system to protect us from them; and a central domain that the English jurist Lord Moulton called "the place of obedience to the unenforceable." Just as important for the preservation of a society is the place of character, good policy, philanthropy, and the love of what is true and right. As this middle territory has shrunk, we have found ourselves caught in the crossfire between freedom on the one side, understood in terms of our individualism (which means that you can do and say anything you want, provided it is not illegal), and the need, on the other hand, to have some controls in society. It is no mystery why America supports seventy percent of the world's lawyers. We have to have litigation to curtail the excesses of our freedom. There is no other way to control this license. The problem, however, is that law cannot do many of the things that character should. We can pass a law against fraud, but we cannot pass a law against lying. We can pass a law against abuse, but we cannot command civility. There are many things that the law cannot do and that character must do. Moral life that is fueled, strengthened, driven, and directed by a serious evangelical theology has a large cultural role to play.

What about church and academy? Wouldn't both benefit from a lively exchange and mutual discussion? Isn't this what Karl Barth did in his *Church Dogmatics,* and weren't the church and the academy both put in his debt? Such a discussion would produce a somewhat different theologian — one who is self-consciously and devotedly within the church, living by the preaching of the Word of God, and loving the God of that Word. This kind of theologian would bring to the academic enterprise a sense of the wonder and greatness of God.

We would see the model not of the pure academic but of the kneeling theologian. Academic culture needs such a model today.

# Contributors

**William J. Abraham** is the Albert Cook Outler Professor of Wesley Studies at Southern Methodist University.

**Alister McGrath** is the Principal of Wycliff Hall at Oxford University.

**Richard Mouw** is President of Fuller Theological Seminary.

**Mark A. Noll** is the McManis Professor of Christian Thought at Wheaton College.

**Cheryl Sanders** is Professor of Christian Ethics at the Howard University School of Divinity.

**Ronald F. Thiemann** is Professor of Theology at Harvard Divinity School.

**David F. Wells** is the Andrew Mutch Distinguished Professor of Historical and Contemporary Theology at Gordon-Conwell Theological Seminary.

**Dallas Willard** is Professor of Philosophy at the University of Southern California at Los Angeles.